EAGER TO LEARN

EAGER
to
LEARN

HELPING CHILDREN BECOME MOTIVATED
AND LOVE LEARNING

Raymond J. Wlodkowski
Judith H. Jaynes

Jossey-Bass Publishers

San Francisco   •   Oxford   •   1991

EAGER TO LEARN
Helping Children Become Motivated and Love Learning
by Raymond J. Wlodkowski and Judith H. Jaynes

Copyright © 1990 by: Jossey-Bass Inc., Publishers
350 Sansome Street
San Francisco, California 94104
&
Jossey-Bass Limited
Headington Hill Hall
Oxford OX3 0BW

Library of Congress Cataloging-in-Publication Data
Wlodkowski, Raymond J., date.
    Eager to learn: helping children become motivated and love
learning / Raymond J. Wlodkowski, Judith H. Jaynes.
        p.   cm.—(A Joint publication in the Jossey-Bass education
series and the Jossey-Bass social and behavioral science series)
    Includes bibliographical references.
    ISBN 1-55542-206-3
    ISBN 1-55542-367-1 (paperback)
    1. Motivation in education. 2. Learning, Psychology of. 3. Home
and school—United States. 4. Education—United States—Parent
participation. I. Jaynes, Judith H. II. Title. III. Series:
Jossey-Bass education series. IV. Series: Jossey-Bass social and
behavioral science series.
LB1065.W58   1990
370.15'4—dc20   89-43456
                                           CIP

Manufactured in the United States of America

The paper in this book meets the guidelines for
permanence and durability of the Committee on
Production Guidelines for Book Longevity of the
Council on Library Resources.

JACKET AND COVER DESIGN BY CHARLOTTE KAY GRAPHIC DESIGN

FIRST EDITION
   HB Printing 10 9 8 7 6 5 4 3
   First paperback printing: August 1991

Code 9014
Code 9180 (paperback)

A joint publication in
THE JOSSEY-BASS EDUCATION SERIES
and
THE JOSSEY-BASS
SOCIAL AND BEHAVIORAL SCIENCE SERIES

To our children:
Katherine,
Claire Elise,
and
Phillip

Contents

Resources

Preface

CURRENTLY, APPROXIMATELY 27 percent of all children in the United States drop out of public school before high school graduation. This troublesome percentage is approaching nearly one out of two students among our ethnic poor. Every teacher knows numerous students who are capable of learning to a far greater extent than they actually do. Since 1980, more than a dozen reports from national panels and commissions that have studied public education in this country agree that the school achievement of our children is below their abilities. In all of these instances, one of the main reasons cited is that many of our children lack motivation to learn in school.

Other national studies that have examined teacher alienation and dissatisfaction report "poor student attitude toward learning" as a major reason for both the physical and psychological withdrawal of teachers from their profession. Recruiting new and able teachers has also suffered because of the appraisal of many college students who see teaching as a difficult career in which one has to work with far too many students who do not want to learn.

Within this dismal picture stand the parents who know only too well the struggle and frequent defeat of trying to make a son or daughter learn. Despite constant badgering and numerous threats, parents end up with disappointing report cards and the very real worry that they are raising a child who does not have the attitude or the skills and knowledge to gain a satisfying life in a very difficult world. All of this often occurs with one more nagging rumination: "What a waste! I should do better. If only I could help my child to work a little harder."

Purpose and Audience

Eager to Learn is a direct attempt to help teachers and parents find realistic ways to help children become motivated to learn. It contains a series of ideas and methods that directly address how to help children to *want* to learn in school, to persevere at learning tasks, to value learning, and to enjoy learning. Whenever possible, this book offers ways to develop in children an intrinsic motivation for learning, which is to find learning itself to be a rewarding activity. We suggest ways to make learning satisfying in all of its aspects, from classwork to doing homework, studying, and even taking tests.

This is the first book of its kind written for both parents and teachers. As Dorothy Rich (*The Forgotten Factor in School Success—The Family*) has written, "The relationship between family and school is comparable to that of the right and left hemispheres of the brain. Both are necessary. Both are complementary, unique, and vital." The more parents can understand and support what teachers do, the more they can help their children. The greater the positive relationship between teachers and parents in what they say and do about children learning, the more powerful their mutual influence can be upon children. Many of the ways to encourage motivation to learn can be sensibly used in both school and home. This book unifies teachers and parents in the best interest of their children's motivation to learn. It is a book to be shared, to be given by parents to teachers and by teachers to parents.

Overview of the Contents

Addressing both parents and teachers, *Eager to Learn* discusses motivation in two parts. Part One deals with how parents and teachers can help to develop motivation to learn as a lifelong personal trait in a child. As we know, some people like to learn in general. They like learning when they are young, and they like to learn when they are older. It appears that such people learn to enjoy learning from their parents and teachers. *Eager to Learn* demonstrates how such learning can be a part of a child's experience in today's families and schools. Part Two of this book deals with solving motivation problems. It discusses what parents and teachers can do to resolve those situations in which students will not attempt certain schoolwork because of anxiety, boredom, or lack of success. It gives specific guidance to parents and teachers to encourage student effort to succeed in school. The chapters in Part Two introduce such skills as problem solving, goal setting, and other strategies that children can use when they want to maintain or increase their own motivation to learn. In this manner, children can learn to rely on themselves as a resource to increase their interest, sense of challenge, or means of gaining more rewarding outcomes.

Because our goal in this book is to communicate with the general population, *Eager to Learn* avoids scholarly jargon and uses direct and descriptive language. Because so much of the book deals with family relations that are strongly influenced by ethnic values, the examples offered are oriented toward the mainstream with the understanding that families and teachers will have to add their own cultural and socioeconomic shadings. Although this book attempts to make the complex topic of motivation clear, it is not a clinical manual designed for helping children with motivational problems stemming from chemical or physical abuse, emotional trauma, or family dysfunction.

Eager to Learn represents our years of experience as parents, teachers, and therapists over the past three decades. Everything we have written has been filtered through each of these three roles and found acceptable. Thus anything we recommend for parents we can also accept as teachers and as therapists, and anything we recommend to teachers we can also accept as parents and as therapists. However, we need to say that no one should take any of our recommendations as an absolute. Motivation to learn is a relatively new field of study in which factual knowledge is difficult to offer with complete certainty. In addition, every child, every teacher, and every parent is unique. Our readers must trust their own judgment regarding the advice we offer. Use it only as it seems reasonable and acceptable to you.

Eager to Learn is for parents and teachers who want to help children and adolescents become motivated and effective learners—people who can learn, who value learning, and who normally find it an enjoyable experience. This book offers parents and teachers a common language and understanding so that they can cooperatively work toward this goal. We discuss motivation as a lifelong trait that can be developed, as well as a specific process that can be increased in particular learning situations. *Eager to Learn* provides a problem-solving approach to situations in which motivation seems to be lacking. It offers concrete, practical suggestions that trust the final judgment of parents and teachers for their application. It is a book that does not treat "love of learning" as a wish or a mere platitude but as a realistic goal that families and schools can reach together.

Acknowledgments

Special thanks are due to Jim Magestro, principal of Parkway Elementary School, Glendale, Wisconsin, and Peter Hays, counselor at the Annie Wright School, Tacoma, Washington, for their insightful comments and thorough review of the first draft of this manuscript. We also want to thank Lynn Luckow, executive editor at Jossey-Bass Inc., Publishers, whose encouragement and faith in our work continued to inspire us throughout the writing of this book. Finally, we want to thank Virginia Nunner and Cheryl Senecal for their masterful job of typing and organizing this manuscript.

Seattle, Washington   Raymond J. Wlodkowski
November 1989   Judith H. Jaynes

The Authors

RAYMOND J. WLODKOWSKI is a faculty member in the graduate program in education at Antioch University in Seattle. He received his B.S. degree (1965) in social science and his Ph.D. degree (1970) in educational and clinical psychology, both from Wayne State University in Detroit. He has been a professor of educational psychology at the University of Wisconsin, Milwaukee, a teacher in the Detroit Public Schools, and a human relations specialist for the Milwaukee Public Schools.

Wlodkowski is a licensed psychologist and certified school psychologist with experience as a family therapist. He is a consultant to national and international organizations, including the Association for Supervision and Curriculum Development, AT&T Communications, and the East Asia Regional Council of Overseas Schools. He is the author of *Motivation and Teaching: A Practical Guide* (1978) and *Enhancing Adult Motivation to Learn* (1985), which received the Phillip E. Frandson Award for Literature. His professional interests and publications are primarily in the areas of human development, instruction, and motivation. He has received the University of Wisconsin, Milwaukee, Award for Teaching Excellence.

JUDITH H. JAYNES is a counselor in the Counseling Center at the University of Puget Sound, Tacoma, Washington, where she also teaches courses in the graduate program in counselor education. In addition, she maintains a private practice as a certified marriage and family therapist. She holds a B.A. degree (1965) in education from San Diego State University, an M.A. degree (1971) in educational psychology from the University of California, Los Angeles, a Ph.D. degree (1978) in urban education from the University of Wisconsin, Milwaukee, and an M.S.W. degree (1983), also from the University of Wisconsin, Milwaukee.

Jaynes is the coauthor (with C. Rugg) of *Adolescents, Alcohol, and Drugs: A Practical Guide for Those Who Work with Young People* (1988). She has made presentations at professional conferences, both national and international, and she has worked as a consultant to schools and social service agencies throughout the United States. Her professional career has included work as an elementary school teacher, a parent education instructor, and director of a number of early childhood education programs.

The central task of education is to implant a will and facility for learning; it should produce not learned but learning people. The truly human society is a learning society, where grandparents, parents, and children are students together.

—Eric Hoffer

Part I

———8———

How Children Become
Motivated to Learn

IS THE IDEA OF A human passion for learning a myth—something society keeps alive as a hope offered to make its schools less dreary and its parents more obliging? We do not think so. Watch a toddler opening a box. Listen to the questions of young children on their first trip to a zoo. Talk with someone about a favorite hobby. Think of all the things you still want to learn. People undertake about eight new learning activities a year.[1] Whether it is finding a better recipe or participating in a job-related workshop, learning is a constant in our lives.

Then there are those people who are obviously more enamored with learning—and they are not all scientists and scholars. They include the trivia buffs, the sports junkies, the reading addicts, and the health nuts; as the labels suggest, they are crazy about learning.

The problem is making learning a constant in educational institutions. Our media bombard us daily with the bad news about higher dropout rates, lower math scores, and greater numbers of children learning less than ever before. Our national concern rises in the face of international competition and the reality that the type of learning that occurs in school—the three R's as well as thinking and problem solving—no longer stops with high school graduation. It continues on the job and in the home. With rapid techno-

1

logical changes and amounts of information progressing exponentially, academic learning will be a way of life in the twenty-first century.

As parents and educators, we are responsible for helping our children to develop motivation to learn that lasts a lifetime and embraces academic learning. This is a complex process for which there are no fixed menus or simple blueprints. But there is information, research, and wisdom about these matters. Because motivation is a relatively recent topic for investigation, the formal knowledge about it can be compared to the first maps describing a new territory. They lead the way, but they are not necessarily complete and may not offer the best routes. Yet anyone who is serious about having a successful journey is bound to study them well beforehand.

The first part of this book represents what we have found to be the most informed and enlightened thinking about what motivation to learn is and how it can be developed in children. The research and ideas we discuss offer a context and conceptual framework for the more practical methods offered in Part Two of this book. By understanding how the culture, the school, the family, and the child form a system of motivational influences, we can be more aware, at every level of society, of how to help children to be both joyful and productive in schools.

Chapter 1

—8—

Motivation:
The Key to Learning

The most important motive for work in the school and in life is the pleasure in work, pleasure in its result and the knowledge of the value of the result to the community.

—Albert Einstein

JEFF'S PARENTS WERE CONSUMED by the delight they had with him as a baby. Never before had watching anyone or anything been so wonderful for them. They followed and celebrated every step of his development with gasps, and applause, and the sure snap of their camera's shutter. His first smile, his first word, and his first step were history-making moments within their family.

Their life with Jeff seemed only to get better as he grew older. His brightness and curiosity as a toddler flowed and merged with their insatiable wonder at his achievements. As a preschooler Jeff was confident and skillful. He could read neighborhood signs with ease, complete commercial jingles on cue, and point out what he called his "favorite words" in any number of books. People told Jeff's parents to have him tested by a psychologist because he seemed so gifted and they should know what his special talents might be. But they did not do this. They wanted Jeff's life to be as normal and as natural as possible. They were grateful for their little boy and felt lucky to be graced with his happy childhood. They knew plenty of parents whose lives with their children were difficult at best. "Let's not tamper with something when it's working," they reassured one another.

3

Jeff entered elementary school like a sturdy ship setting off on a smooth sea. He was sure of himself. He made friends easily. He did well in all subjects. His teachers liked him. Jeff's parents looked forward to parent-teacher conferences. They were like small meetings of a mutual admiration society. Everyone thought everyone else was wonderful. There were some criticisms now and then—tardy homework, careless spelling, messy handwriting—but nothing really serious, nothing more than the necessary refinements of a good student.

It was not until the sixth grade that Jeff's parents felt their first twinge of a definite threat to their son's motivation to learn in school. Jeff received his first D on a report card. It was in math. His parents were upset. They talked with each other about it before they talked with Jeff. Maybe Jeff was slacking. Maybe it was a fluke. Maybe they weren't paying enough attention to Jeff's schoolwork. Maybe their son wasn't capable in math. Maybe it was a poor teacher. Jeff told them he didn't like math. It was boring and the teacher was a tough grader.

When Jeff's parents went to see his math teacher, Ms. Bartlett, they were a little anxious. She was friendly but seemed tired and abrupt. Yes, Jeff could do better. Yes, he was capable. His problem was that he was not concentrating and that he was not completing his homework. The parents did not argue with the teacher. Neither of them voiced a nagging doubt that maybe Ms. Bartlett was not making the subject interesting for their son. When they later confided this to one another, they admitted they felt uncomfortable and didn't know how to say it without starting a fight. They did tell Jeff he had to shape up in math and get all his work done for the class. Jeff didn't argue. He seemed resigned to obey them but with a sullenness they had not before seen in him. For the rest of the year he received C's in math.

Now, in the ninth grade, Jeff's schoolwork has taken a real tumble. He has started getting F's for the first time. His parents have become adept at arguing with teachers. They can say what is bothering them, but this does not seem to help the situation. The teachers do not seem to change and neither do Jeff's parents. In fact, a predictable pattern has emerged. As each side complains to the other, both sides seem to lose confidence in helping Jeff and trusting one another.

In the meantime, learning in school has become a kind of tug-of-war between Jeff and his parents. They pull him in to learning by threatening and badgering him. This forces him temporarily to do better in his schoolwork and his grades rise slightly. However, when his parents ease the pressure, he seems to slide back a bit further from his studies. In fact, he is interested in almost anything but schoolwork—friends, television, sports, music, and any number of other distractions. Jeff's parents do not like pressuring their son. They realize they are winning hollow victories. They know that the older their son gets, the less they can coerce him into learning. It is agonizing for them to remember Jeff as a young child, so eager to learn, so motivated in school. They worry. They still believe there must be a way. They haven't given up.

We begin this book with this unsettling story because although it may not exactly represent any student, or family, or teacher, it contains many of the common elements and inevitable questions that make children's motivation to learn in school worrisome for well-intentioned parents and teachers. Let us more directly list some of these factors:

- Why do most children seem so curious and motivated to learn when they are very young, but seem to lose their passion for learning as they grow older and progress through school?
- Why do parents who care for their children and offer them stable and loving homes often have problems with maintaining the motivation of their children to learn?
- Because we know so much about learning, why have we not created some formula or plan to rear children in a way that will help them love to learn throughout their lives?
- Why do most children seem less motivated to learn math and science than other subjects in school?
- Should we force our children to learn if we believe that is best for them?
- Why are television programs and sports, often presented in a simple-minded fashion, so appealing to people?

- Who have a greater influence on children's motivation to learn—parents or teachers?
- How can teachers be trained to know how to motivate children to learn what they are teaching?
- How can parents and teachers work more effectively together to help children to want to learn?
- How can motivation to learn the subjects taught in school be restored or rejuvenated in young people who no longer seem to care?

Many of the answers to these questions are essential to providing a better education for our children. Yet there are no short, simple, or unqualified responses. The rest of this book is our answer. To begin, we can ask, What is motivation to learn and why is it so important?

In the broadest sense, motivation to learn is a value and a desire for learning. This understanding is the platform for the main goal of this book: *to help children value learning.* This means the child is not only willing to learn but also cherishes and enjoys the act of learning, as well as the outcome of learning. This can occur inside or outside of school. In this sense, the child likes the solving of the math problem as much as the achievement of the correct solution or appreciates the process of writing a composition as much as any grade it might be given.

The child who values learning is truly gifted because that child is becoming a lifelong learner. This is a child who is attracted to reading, writing, thinking, calculating, and problem solving. This student has a natural bent to do those things that will lead to occupational success in the twenty-first century and contribute to the positive evolution of society. Such a student becomes an adult who is often capable of excellence because the best in science, scholarship, or art cannot be coerced from an unwilling mind or heart.

This kind of learner is graced with a perspective that makes the difficult desirable; this is the true benefit of motivation to learn. Learning is often extremely difficult and risky. We may not be able to learn something well, and we often do not know this until we have tried for some time without success. However, this pattern of futile attempts and excessive effort also often precedes great discoveries (Edison and the light bulb) as well as everyday academic progress (successful writing). Diligence and endurance within a framework of a love for learning ennoble the human spirit.

Acquiring and Maintaining Motivation to Learn

Virtually all children are born with motivation to learn.[1] It is a characteristic of the human species. Children are naturally curious explorers. Infants search their environment to make sense of it. Toddlers ramble awkwardly but with determination, pushing and pulling everything in sight to find out what "it" does. Preschoolers are fascinated and awestruck by the new and different in their world. Parents know that the very young inhabit a galaxy filled with wonder and have a voracious appetite for learning.

And then comes school. Too often, the child's motivation to learn seems to dwindle with age. Reminders to study seem to replace the frequent spontaneous applause that accompanied the learning conquests of early childhood. During adolescence, these reminders can often become threats that promise ill will to the child whose report card does not measure up to the expectations of parents. In too many homes the topic of learning has become a tense subject, the leading edge of a combat zone where parents battle to coerce their children into learning. Children retaliate with the guerrilla warfare of sullen rebelliousness, and both parties fear the next report card.

What has happened? Where did the motivation go? Why does it often seem to languish as children go through school? There are many reasons why this depletion in motivation to learn can occur. Some combination in the number, degree, and quality of the following reasons probably contributes to this decline of motivation to learn.

1. Learning in school occurs in groups with a formalized curriculum and a constantly applied grading system. No longer is the child alone and under the care of a parent who is thrilled and eager to entertain any whimsical curiosity that might be displayed in school. The child is now a learner among as many as thirty-five more learners, all needing some attention and following a textbook or set of materials programmed in a sequence that most often demands far more flexibility in the child than in its own format. Then there is the grading, relentless and intrusive in American schools—daily quizzes, weekly tests, midsemester exams, final exams, grades on assignments, homework, and projects, sometimes competitively given, sometimes absolute.[2] To receive a grade means to have the outward evidence of learning evaluated, often judged in comparison with others, and marked in a ledger. Failures and poor marks do not fade away. They are counted against the student. And with every year, as the necessity for a college education looms larger on the horizon, the currency for college entrance, the cumulative grade-point average, rises in value and puts pressure on students.

Toddlers do not face this reality. No one would ever think of improving a poorly enunciated "da-da" by grading it. Imagine what might happen to the joy of cooking if the recipients of a meal graded it upon each occasion. "Your roast beef is only about a C, but don't worry; your gravy deserves a B. However, if I compare it with your neighbor's cooking, I'll have to lower the entire meal by half a grade." Sounds ridiculous, doesn't it? Yet most children face this kind of thinking in their daily school lives. Grading does little to sustain a deeply felt desire for learning for the sake of learning.

2. *The acquisition of advanced knowledge and skill is complex, demanding, and time-consuming, especially for the less talented.* Reading and understanding a Shakespearean play is not the same as reading and understanding an Aesop fable, and solving a problem in calculus is not the same as solving a problem in long division. Although these comparisons may suggest differences in complexity, acquiring and displaying advanced knowledge or skill involves much more than the word *complexity* can describe. Let us take writing as a general example. Advanced writing would be publishable writing, something that might appear in a national magazine. This might mean an essay or story about something interesting to the public. It would have to display thinking that is insightful or original or at least stimulating. The piece would have to be written well. To accomplish these goals, the writer would have to do research and a good deal of rewriting to shape the material into final form. All of this demands time, energy, concentration, reflection, critical thinking, and a final product that is clear and well organized. As students move along in any academic discipline,

the subject requires more of the learner and is less forgiving of error because competence is expected. For many learners, their journey into the advanced areas of greater knowledge reaches a point of diminishing returns.[3] More time and effort do not reduce their errors to an extent that allows them to feel successful, and they become discouraged.

3. Motivation, in general, is a limited supply of energy that must be judiciously dispensed among ourselves and our world.[4] Everything in and around us, including our minds and our feelings, competes for our motivation. It is difficult to do more than one thing at a time competently. Whenever we pay attention to something, it usually means not paying attention to something else, whether it be our jobs, our children, or this book.

The finite nature of human motivation in a complex and demanding world has profound consequences. It means that every day we must make choices and decisions about how we will dispense our time, energy, and attention. To a certain extent, habits, routines, and priorities ease the burden of these decisions. They act as the traffic signals, speed limits, and known destinations in the travels of our daily lives. They help to maintain focus and harmony in our everyday existence. Yet as natural as they may seem, they have been determined in large part by the necessities of living (food, rest, and work, for example) and the values we have learned (friendship, honesty, perseverance). In this arena, motivation to learn must find a place along with motivation to play, motivation to ᴜe a good friend, and all the other motivations that exist and are born in the developing lives of children. And the more that motivation to learn becomes a part of a habit, a routine, and a priority in children's lives, the more effectively and harmoniously they will learn in a place called school.

Thus we can view motivation to learn as an internal guidance system that attempts to maintain a child's focus in the direction of learning but must stand on its own and compete against all the other attractions of daily existence. Let's look at how difficult this can be.

Professional athletes are among the most adulated and rewarded people in the United States. Some National Basketball Association players make over a million dollars a year. They play a wonderful game in front of thousands of adoring fans led by cheer-leaders. Television cameras record their movements, every one of which is commented on by enthusiastic sportscasters for audiences that can swell into the tens of millions. These athletes have a chance to make the playoffs and reap thousands more dollars. Even if their team loses, they can eventually become free agents and sell their skills to the highest bidders. Their pictures adorn the daily local sports pages, their game statistics are printed in newspapers all over the world, and they have chances to make still more money by en-dorsing commercial products ranging from shaving cream to syrup. Yet with all of these motivational realities and potentialities, we constantly read about coaches who cannot "motivate" these men to play basketball with intensity and effort. Why?

Because motivation that is acquired through learning—such as to play basketball, or to manage a shop, or to teach a class—can be extraordinarily unstable. Just one of many possible distractions can command a person's interest and spoil his or her intentions: a family problem, a physical ache, a financial investment, an over-heated room, a forthcoming vacation, or a home fixture in need of repair. These and any of a hundred other everyday occurrences can break your concentration, change your mood, or divert your eyes from the mark. That is the way of this type of motivation. It can be gone in a second.

Motivation that derives from physiological needs such as hunger and thirst does not as easily fall prey to distraction. Our bodies continue to send the message that we need to do something because our basic survival is at stake.

Motivation to learn begins as a natural inclination in human beings, but is eventually shaped in such a way that it continually becomes not only the cause and the mediator of learning but the result of learning as well. In this way it acts more like an attitude. Motivation to learn is extremely vulnerable to the distractions of daily existence. As children grow older, their world widens and the environment offers more and more powerful competitors that moti-vation to learn may not be able to overcome: television, peer groups, and the streets, to name a few.

In addition, eventually there is something called adolescence, which in the United States is a culture unto itself. It has its own language, its own medium (MTV), its own dress code, its own geography (malls, cars, and so forth), and its own financial support (teens command billions of dollars in this society). So often within this culture motivation to learn in an academic sense is incompatible with the attractions of this generation's more notorious elements (the drug culture, gangs). There is no question that as children grow older in a free society, they encounter many compelling distractions that can draw them away from academics and diminish the power of their motivation to learn in school.

No children totally escape these three potential diminishers of motivation to learn: (1) the design of the graded school, (2) the increasing complexity of advanced learning, and (3) the enormous attractions and distractions of a buzzing, often chaotic, world. They know no ethnic, social, or class boundaries. Taken together, these forces amount to a climatic shift in how much formal learning appeals to students. Stormy is not too strong a word to describe the present relationship between many of our young people and learning. Just as adults cooperate to protect their children's well-being in severe weather, so must teachers and parents join together to ensure that the desire for learning among their children is not swept away.

Chapter 2

Family, School, Culture: Powerful Influences

Human history becomes more and more a race between educa- tion and catastrophe.

—H. G. Wells

SOMETHING FOR PARENTS AND TEACHERS to consider always is that as a child grows older, motivation to learn is undergoing a transforma- tion from a natural state of curiosity and wonder into something resembling a personal trait as ever present as honesty or intelli- gence. Motivation to learn permeates the entire school life of the child. As we said earlier, it is a cause, a mediator, and a result of learning. Over a lifetime, it is the human framework that can ensure acquiring whatever skills are necessary to obtain cherished goals.

Motivation to learn can take many forms and eventually will become a personal characteristic that is largely determined through the process of learning. Children literally learn to be interested in math, fascinated by science, and intrigued with art. They can also learn to be interested in drugs, fascinated by violence, and intrigued with gambling. Young people's motivation to learn does not disap- pear, but it can develop in ways that lead them to better themselves and society—or not.

This book advocates helping children develop a motivation to learn, *largely in the educational sense*—that is, to value and pursue reading, writing, thinking, computing, problem solving, and the like.

When a child's motivation to learn is well developed as a personal trait, the future is blessed with discovery, opportunity, and contributions. For these young individuals, going to college is a natural step; on-the-job training is desirable, and alternative vocations are realistically possible. People who possess motivation to learn may find external barriers of circumstance and prejudice, but they are not their own enemies and they are the most fit *to learn* ways to overcome such obstacles.

In fact, some of the best historical examples of such people in this country are its early pioneers and explorers. Meriwether Lewis and William Clark come readily to mind. While still youthful (both men were in their early thirties) and having had established careers in the military, they conducted an adventure into learning where their educational skills were as valuable as their courage. Seeking a water route to the Pacific Ocean, they traveled more than 4,000 miles through unknown territory for over two years. In our opinion, their most amazing feat was their legacy, a collection of journals and maps so articulate, so accurate, and so filled with learning and wonder that they formed the informational foundation and fueled the inspiration of people moving west for the rest of the nineteenth century. Lewis and Clark are exemplary models of motivation to learn in both a figurative and literal sense because the frontier for our youth is more mental than physical. What our children learn is what they will become; their minds, not their bodies, have the greatest distances to travel.

Major Influences on Motivation to Learn

There are four major influences on a child's motivation to learn: the culture, the family, the school, and the child himself or herself. Each major influence represents a system. We will discuss how each system appears to exert influence from a perspective that includes the psychological, sociological, anthropological, and historical viewpoint.

Culture. Every ethnic group has stated and implied values regarding learning in the academic or traditional sense. These values are transmitted through such avenues as the dominant religion, the myths and folklore of the culture, the political legislation for education, the status and pay of teachers, and the expectations for parents regarding the preparation of their children for school and their role in relationship to the school. Culture also has much to say about what rewards for learning students should seek and expect.

In recent years, the United States has witnessed exceptionally high academic achievement by Asian/Pacific Americans, which far outdistances the relative proportion of their numbers in our society.[1] Culture appears to have much to do with this circumstance. In addition to this phenomenon, Japan is continuously heralded in our popular press for its technological advances, economic wealth, and the scholastic achievement of its children. Taking a closer look at the Japanese culture as it relates to learning and education offers one brief example of how powerful an influence culture as a system can be.

The Japanese culture places a high value on educational success, and achievement in school is seen as strongly related to personal virtue.[2] This view is woven into the very fabric of Japanese cultural values. Learning in school is a moral issue, and when a student exerts intense effort in academic pursuits, this reflects positively on the student as well as on the student's family. In fact, this demonstration of hard work is an important part of the tapestry. Success that is easily derived is not as highly regarded. The most highly esteemed accomplishments are those that are seen to result from the concerted efforts, over time, of both the student and the family. Studies indicate that Japanese mothers and their children emphasize effort more than ability, compared to American mothers and their children, as a primary means to good school performance.[3]

In response to this important belief system, parental involvement in children's lives is deep and much investment of time and energy takes place, literally, from conception on. *Taikyo* ("education in the womb") is a firmly established tradition in Japan. This implies providing positive environmental influences prior to birth as well as after. Both direct and indirect learning by children is taken extremely seriously. Consequently, educational decisions are based on much thought and consideration.

In Japanese society, the education of children receives a top priority. Parents are committed to institutional efforts to educate their children, and teachers receive considerable respect and support from them. Thus for Japanese students a unity exists among culture, family, and school that powerfully nurtures their motivation to learn.

The Family. Based on the research to date, as well as our own clinical experience, parents appear to be the primary influence on a child's motivation to learn.[4] Their formative effect on their children's motivation to learn has an impact at every stage of development, lasting through the high school years and beyond.

The research of Benjamin Bloom supplies vivid evidence for this kind of impact.[5] His research team conducted in-depth interviews with talented and very successful young professionals (ages twenty-eight to thirty-five) who are highly recognized in difficult, competitive fields, including research mathematics, neurology, classical piano, and tennis. He found that the most common characteristic of their general education, specialized training, and subsequent achievement was enthusiastic parent involvement. Even when the accomplishment and expertise of these young people excluded their parents' direct involvement, they saw their parents' support as the main reference point reinforcing their goals as worthwhile and within their reach.

The fact that parents' enthusiastic involvement was the most common characteristic among Bloom's subjects, who varied widely in ethnicity and socioeconomic status, increases in significance in the light of the research of Reginald Clark.[6] Dr. Clark has spent more than a decade studying well-motivated high achievers, at both the high school and grade school levels, who came from low-income families. His research leads him to the conclusion that what makes the difference for such students is that they come from "effective families":

Like effective schools, effective families have a set of easy-to-identify characteristics. These cut across family income, education, and ethnic background. They remain true for single- and two-parent households and for families with working and non-working mothers. Effective families display a number of positive attitudes and behaviors toward their children which help them to succeed in school and in life.[7]

Clark lists the following characteristics of effective families:[8]

1. *A feeling of control over their lives:* Effective parents believe they can make a difference in their children's academic and personal development. They do not feel overwhelmed by their circumstances. Even when they live in poverty, they keep a hopeful, reassuring outlook. They do not feel sorry for themselves. They not only listen attentively to the problems of their own children, they also have time for others. Children know their homes are a safe place to gather for support and understanding.

2. *A frequent communication of high expectations to children:* They believe their children are personally responsible for attending classes, listening carefully, and participating actively in order to learn. Their parental folk wisdom says, "You have to go to school if you want to get ahead." Although they do not *demand* that their children continue schooling beyond twelfth grade, they frequently emphasize their expectation that their children will participate in some form of secondary education or training. Their children know that wanting to be successful in school is the reasonable and right attitude to have.

3. *A family dream of success for the future:* They have a vision of personal success for each child and a plan for making their dreams come true. The dream that most families contemplate combines good health and material well-being (a good job, nice home) with an active spiritual life and service to the community. They talk with their children about the specific steps they can take both now and later to realize their dream. Their children know that getting a good education is a major part of this plan.

4. *A view of hard work as a key to success:* Effective parents tell their children, in many ways, that personal effort is the key to success. They emphasize that it is not primarily fate or genes

or good looks that make the difference but specifically hard work. Their children believe that success will come from their own inner motivation and commitment.

5. *An active, not a sedentary, life-style:* They discourage idleness and help guide their children's time into wholesome activities. They are continually on the lookout for academic development programs and part-time work for their children. They encourage their children to take advantage of school and community resources. These parents know where their children are and whom they are with; they encourage them to associate with children who have similar values regarding work and school. Their children tend to view life as something you participate in to give as well as receive its blessings.

6. *Twenty-five to thirty-five home-centered learning hours per week:* Some of these hours include time devoted to homework or leisure-time reading. But these families view learning more broadly and consider such activities as hobbies, games, household chores, part-time jobs, sports, organized youth programs, family outings, and even creative daydreaming as constructive.

7. *A view of the family as a mutual support system and problem-solving unit:* From the early years, effective parents give every child some household responsibility appropriate to his or her age. Often, in single-parent and two-career families, older children act as advisers to their younger brothers and sisters. Children realize they are needed by and can contribute to their families.

8. *Clearly understood household rules, consistently enforced:* Effective parents justify the limits and sanctions they set by citing ethical standards (the Golden Rule, for example) or superior knowledge (their own experience). In disputes or conflicts, they usually give their children opportunities to find resolutions, and generally proceed in a fair and loving way. In general, they put more energy into finding worthwhile activities for their children than into keeping their children in line. Their children feel accepted and responsible for their actions.

9. *Frequent contact with teachers:* They are likely often to be involved in parent-teacher groups and school activities. They

check on their children's progress and generally cooperate with teachers. They want to know how they can support school lessons through home activities. The children see their parents and teachers as a unified force helping them to be successful in school.

10.   *An emphasis on spiritual growth:* They encourage and inspire children to strive for inner peace and love. They connect satisfying personal needs with the use of talents and energies to help others. The children believe they can gain the strength to overcome fears and handle conflicts and stress.

It seems obvious that parents should make the biggest difference in the development of a child's motivation to learn. Research findings such as those cited earlier are supportive and insightful but not unexpected. Parents are the first and most important teachers in a child's life. We model and interpret the world for our children. With each child, we get about eighteen years to do this. We show our children what to care about, what to find funny, and what to believe in. We nurture or undermine their trust and self-confidence. It is difficult to precisely assess our impact on our children, but what matters is doing the best job we can for the time we have with our children. It is within the capability of most families to do this well, however we define *family*.

School. When it comes to motivation to learn, teachers do make a difference. In most cases, they are not as powerful as parents, but they can make school life miserable or appealing. Each of us can remember a teacher who filled the classroom with excitement and hope and opened doors for us to find knowledge fascinating.

How does a teacher do this? Is it the magic of personality? Are motivating teachers simply born, and are we destined to hope and pray that our children will have the good fortune to meet a few during their school years?

Both research and clinical experience offer testimony that teachers who enhance the motivation of their students are everyday people who share professional behaviors that can be learned and possess characteristics that are largely under their own control.[9]

One of the traits of motivating teachers is enthusiasm.[10] They care about what they teach and communicate to their students that what they are learning is important. Such teachers offer living proof of this and are apt models whose intensity beckons identification and inspiration. But enthusiasm is born less of one's genes than of a sense of purpose, an enjoyment of sharing knowledge, professional pride, and the responsiveness of students.

However, if enthusiasm alone were enough to be a motivating teacher, then the classic example of a good teacher would probably be Donald Duck rather than Mr. Chips. It takes much more than energy to enhance the motivation of students. Let's look at some of the other qualities of effective, motivating teachers.

They are good managers.[11] They can handle a class and keep it moving. Students feel safe with them and can concentrate on the work at hand.

They expect students to be successful learners.[12] All students get a chance to learn and are held accountable. Students know their teachers will not give up on them.

They present material to students that is within their capacity to learn.[13] Students know that *with effort* they can learn and complete assignments.

They offer corrective feedback to students.[14] On important assignments and learning tasks, motivating teachers show students what their mistakes are and how they can find a way to help themselves. Students know these teachers will help them to improve.

They give fair tests.[15] The students know when all important exams are expected and the criteria for grading them. Students also know how to prepare for their tests and have a reasonable chance to demonstrate the knowledge or skill requested.

They give grades that are informative.[16] Students can understand the criteria used to establish their grades and know why they have received the mark that they have been given.

They challenge and stimulate.[17] Students sense that they are pursuing learning that is at least moderately difficult and realize that they are using their minds in new and different ways.

They help students to realize their growing competence and mastery.[18] They make comments, both verbal and written, that let students know that their learning is the result of efforts for which the students are personally responsible, such as determination, perseverance, creativity, and the like. Students know they are becoming more effective at what they value.

They are empathic.[19] Effective teachers consider the students' viewpoints. Students believe these teachers are sensitive to their needs and perspectives.

They value knowledge over grades.[20] They set a tone that learning is what counts. Students know that these teachers will not reject them because their grades or scores are less than those of someone else.

Being a teacher who enhances the motivation of students to learn is clearly a demanding job. To enact the qualities and carry out the skills just noted for 35 students in elementary school or 100 or more in middle school and high school is frequently less a question of competence than an issue of finding time and forestalling exhaustion! To a crucial extent, the teacher's influence on the students' motivation to learn depends on the attitudes and traits that the students carry into the classroom.

The Child. When it comes to nurturing excellence in learning, most teachers will only be as successful as their students will let them be. Master teachers at the highest levels of any profession, whether it be music, medicine, or sports, know this. They have selection systems that bring to them the best of the brightest—only the most capable and the most motivated students. Nothing less is acceptable to them.

In some ways, teaching is like farming. Both nurture growth. Both to some extent depend on the quality of the life-giving elements that they are cultivating. There is a point at which a farmer *alone* cannot overcome the negative effects of poor soil or harmful weather. He may need help through irrigation and soil nutrients. There also is a point at which a teacher *alone* cannot overcome the negative effectives of hostile behavior and self-defeating attitudes in a student. However, just what that point may be and to what extent the child's attitude and behavior block the skillful effort of a *united parent and teacher committed to the child's well-being* is not fully known.

Hope for the farmer lies in knowing first what a successful and healthy crop is and then in realizing how it came to be. Hope for parents and teachers working together lies in a similar direction.

So let us begin by looking at what a successful and healthy student appears to be.

Today, many people seem to view the attainment of a hefty grade-point average and peak scores on the Scholastic Achievement Test as the ultimate indicators of being a successful student. We certainly think such accomplishments are noteworthy. Yet we are concerned that the current American obsession with such signs of achievement has reached a point of diminishing returns and harmful influence.[21]

Such gross emphasis on scores and grades as the most important aims and reflections of learning narrows the benefits of learning and pressures students to seek the most expedient means to external recognition of what they have learned. In short, it leads them on a steady path to joyless learning. In the throes of such a miserly vision, students have to work very hard to avoid becoming cynical about the higher purposes of a decent education.

There are far too many students who achieve well in school but whose motivational profile is mainly an unfortunate configuration of pressure, anxiety, guilt, worry, and self-imposed coercion. They resemble young workaholics who are tensely driven and ever mindful of the next indicator of their achievement. Tears, depression, and eating disorders are too often also a part of their psychological portrait.

Can students take learning seriously, do well, and still enjoy it? Yes! Students who are most likely to accomplish this have the following characteristics and behaviors:[22]

- They get good grades but tend to see them as concise information about the quality of their learning rather than symbols of their identity.
- They are intrinsically motivated, finding the process of learning (reading, studying) to be satisfying.
- They generally have accepted the learning values of their family and school.
- They are self-regulated learners. They generally prepare, organize, and study under their own guidance and determination. (But they are not free from needing parental guidance and nudging once in a while.)

- They realize that they are mainly responsible for their own learning. They tend not to blame others when learning does not go smoothly.
- They realize the benefits of effort. They know they have to strive for improvement and excellence.
- They are good problem solvers. They know how to use resources, such as the library, and to ask for help when they need it.
- They have moments of doubt and are vulnerable to anxiety about certain exams, but these incidents are not excessive, frequent, or immobilizing.
- They see their setbacks in learning more as information than as failure. They more often than not truly do learn from their mistakes.

The best of all possible worlds for the development of motivation to learn is when there is harmony among all four areas of influence. If the culture values effort as a necessary part of learning and the family and school are in total agreement in their support of this value, the children will know, accept, and identify with this same value. They will see it as the natural way to be, modeling and reflecting it within the family and school to which they belong.

However, our culture is made up of many ethnic groups in a time of rapid transformation. Families and schools have been changing dramatically in the past twenty years. Unity of values regarding motivation to learn is probably the remotest it has ever been. In addition, the four systems are not equal in their influence.

The student who values learning and possesses the characteristics just described comes from a family that has helped to make this so. Parents and teachers working together can more effectively nurture a desire for learning in more students. How to do this so that it will last a lifetime is the focus of our next chapter.

Chapter 3

Eagerness to Learn: Cultivating the Desire

Treat people as if they were what they ought to be and you help them become what they are capable of being.

—Johann von Goethe

IF LOVE OF LEARNING has not taken hold within most children by the time of high school graduation, it is very unlikely it ever will. This is not so much a disenchantment as much as it is a curse. People who do not like learning can be professionally successful. But when it comes to reading, writing, and computing, they have to push and coerce themselves as they might to visit a dentist.

Because motivation to learn is an enduring trait, parents and teachers can help to develop it as they might also nurture courage or self-reliance within a child. Sometimes the growth of motivation to learn is unseen or appears dormant for prolonged periods of time. Adolescence can be an especially unstable time for outward signs that a child cares about learning.[1] We mention this because we take a never-give-up attitude toward children. Call it a leap of faith. Call it stubbornness. Call it naivete. We simply believe that all that grows within children may not be apparent to them or to those who care most about them. The harvest of the mind and spirit is often least evident to willful observation.

In this chapter, we will discuss the guidelines for developing within children a lifelong motivation to learn. This trait can take an entire childhood and adolescence to establish. No one knows exactly when parents can sit back and say, "Now it is up to them.

We've done our share." In addition, each guideline is open to cultural and familial interpretation. For example, there are many different and effective ways to show gratitude. It can be nonverbal or verbal (a nod of the head or a thank-you), short or long (a brief salute or a lengthy speech), and private or public (at home or at a banquet). We can say the same for *communicating positive expectations to a child,* which is one of our guidelines for developing motivation to learn. There are many different ways to do this, from a hand on the shoulder before your child leaves for school on the day of an important test to a discussion of an adolescent's aspirations for a college education.

So take what we offer and put it into your own words and your own ways. See our examples as models to use as inspirations for your own creations.

Because both parents and teachers influence a child's motivation to learn, we follow each guideline for the parent with a guideline for the teacher covering the same general goal. This format should encourage mutual support between parents and teachers; both have something to do that directly benefits how the other is helping the child.

It also shows how effective teaching frequently is an extension of effective parenting. Finally, our guidelines offer ideas that parents and teachers can use to work together to help the child develop a lasting value for learning.

Treat your child as a person continuously growing toward increased self-direction and effectiveness. This guideline covers a number of attitudes and behaviors that together are based on what researchers have found to be the parental styles most frequently associated with positive attitudes toward learning and school success.[2] Respected researchers have used such labels as "sponsored independence," "authoritative," and "autonomous" to describe these parental ways of treating children.

Our work as teachers and therapists strongly supports their findings and suggests that as parents we should view our children as capable of making decisions, understanding limits, and guiding their own behavior according to rules appropriate for their age. Therefore, we set and enforce a bottom line where necessary, such as coming home by a certain time, doing particular household chores,

or finishing assigned homework. However, such directives are offered with sensible reasons and trust that our children can handle
the situation without excessive pressure and monitoring. We respect
and listen to the viewpoints of our children because their opinions
and perspectives inform us and contribute to better understanding.

We realize that our children are going to need to practice
thinking about their own behavior and learn that the choices they
make lead to consequences. They create results through their own
decisions. By giving our children chances to guide themselves within the limits where their judgment is sound, we help them to build
self-confidence because they will have repeated successes for which
they know they are responsible. By listening to our children, we
show them that they can understand and make judgments about
their world that are trustworthy, and this allows them to increase
their own capacity to trust themselves. For example, children of elementary school age can begin to make decisions about how much
time is needed to clean their rooms and what kind of help they may
need to complete a particular homework assignment.

In at least three very important ways, such treatment of children develops motivation to learn. The first way is to increase the
child's identification with the parents' values: The child can see that
he or she is a real part of the family that establishes and carries out
those values. Thus when the family values are a respect and a love of
learning, the child is naturally attracted to them.

The second outcome is that such treatment helps to develop
attitudes and habits of self-direction, and most of learning—90 percent in our opinion—is self-directed. No one is going to sit next to
our children the rest of their lives and help them to study, to do
quality work, to think, and to make the extra effort that develops
excellent skills. That is a job only the self can accomplish, and the
self needs practice to make such habits of self-regulation automatic
responses.

The third benefit is that children learn to look to themselves
for what happens to them. They determine most of what they accomplish, and this is obvious to them because they have a voice in
what goes on in their own family and can see how their growing
ability extends the boundaries of their lives. Learning makes sense

because it extends the limits of their skills, and children realize they are going to need knowledge to enjoy and contribute to their world.

The teacher's role in this regard is to set standards and limits in terms of both academics and discipline that can be supported with fair-minded reasoning.[3] When problems occur in school, children need to be asked to use their values and judgment to help solve them. Teachers who involve children this way help students to realize they have some degree of choice and control about much of what they do in school. Such teacher actions may include allowing students to select topics to be studied, to plan projects, to learn in cooperative groups, and to practice to reduce mistakes. Teachers may also employ such methods as contracts and goal setting to encourage academic progress. Such teachers are approachable and willing to listen to the student (but realize this may be extremely limited because time is so tightly budgeted in a school day). In general, they foster a willingness to learn rather than a blind submission to their own authority. Such teachers readily offer prompt, informative feedback on tests and assignments to help students realize that they are responsible for their progress in learning, much as the screen of the microcomputer lets the users know that they are in control of what happens next on the monitor.

Actively model and share a value for learning. It is cliché, but it is so powerful: When it comes to learning, practicing what we preach is essential. The fantastic thing about this understanding is that there are so many ways to do it. In addition to repeating common suggestions we will add a few more that parents and teachers reading this book can adapt to their personal styles.

As Frank Smith has written, "Nothing attracts young people more than activities, abilities, or secrets that absorb adults."[4] Children want to know about the things we find worthwhile. As parents, we can engage them in three different ways as we routinely pursue our daily lives. Reading, math, and science will serve as our examples.

The first way is as a model to our children. "Giving a good example" is a basic value in every major religion throughout the world, and it is no less true for establishing a lifelong motivation to learn. What our children see and hear us do is probably the most lasting of everything they learn from us. Reading is easy to model.

Our delight and immersion in newspapers, magazines, and books is simple to display. But what about arithmetic? Here we must be more careful because what our children see at home may be more negative than positive.

In this culture, numbers and math are frequently associated with pain and frustration. Unbalanced checkbooks, unpaid bills, unforeseen debts, and unfathomable IRS forms plague many a family. Dealing with money is the most common use of numbers and computations in our society, and their relationship may be too often unbalanced toward words and actions that say numbers are difficult to understand. We agree with the literature that says innumeracy is epidemic in our society.[5] Thus we offer the only commandment in this book: "In front of children, thou shalt not use numbers in vain." We can stress our numerically oriented successes in correct measures in cooking, fertilizing, and sewing; accurate estimates in savings, weather, and sports; and problem solving in hobbies, tax deductions, and home repairs. A parent who buys a few shares of stock for or with a child and then participates in following gains and losses will help demystify fractions and percentages. Helping a child with a coin or stamp collection is another way to play with numbers and also to learn geography. On the other side of the ledger, we can temper our public display of math ineptitude. ("I'm just no good at math," an unfortunately common refrain, promotes self-defeating attitudes.)

For those of us who believe our scientific understanding to be minimal, displaying a keen interest in science may seem hardly possible. Yet the natural attraction of our wonder and respect for science can serve as a magnet to attract our children toward involvement with this subject. The media afford us opportunities at every turn. Public television has wonderful science series, such as "Nova." Magazines and newspapers abound with weekly and daily reports of scientific advancements. Our comments of interest in such matters as the weather or the plants and animals in our gardens and parks can lead our children to seek out the mysteries that science, by its very nature, is always a part of.

The second way to model and share our value for learning is to make the child a beneficiary of our joyful use of the fundamentals of learning. The most obvious example is to read to our children (which we advocate at any age) on a regular basis. To share the usefulness of writing, we can include a positive note in our children's lunch bags or on their dressers or help them compose a thank-you note for a gift from a relative. When it comes to arithmetic, there are many opportunities in the care and feeding of our children: taking their temperature, measuring their growth in height and weight, contributing to their savings, and portioning their dessert, to name a few. The main thing is to let our children see, at any age, how math helps us to understand the world in beneficial ways. The same could be said for science as well. Every time we repair a bicycle or a broken toy for our children, we are using tools, technology, chemicals, and principles that are part of our scientific legacy. Our treatment of their injuries and illnesses is another area where medical science is part of the entire process. In general, in ways that are not overbearing, we want to let our children know that the essentials of such academic subjects as math and science are a very real part of how we behave as good parents.

The third way to model and share our value for learning is to make the child a partner or collaborator in our own learning and application of academic skills.[6] The key word is *together:* read something delightful together, write a poem together, repair something technical together, cook something delicious together, save something important together. For parents and children, this is probably the most satisfying as well as impressive way to influence our children's motivation to learn. If we think of our own lives, of what we shared with our parents, the things we accomplished together, these are valued moments, times without regret in which we could see the world through their eyes and come to understand it for ourselves. Now we have this chance with our own children.

For the teacher who wants to actively model and share a value for learning, one word sums it all up—*enthusiasm.* By their very presence, enthusiastic teachers tell students that they care about what they are teaching, and this value radiates through them with vitality. This gives the subject credibility because such teachers are living testimony to the worth of their discipline. They can inspire students who are looking for adults whose beliefs and approach to their vocation say, without words, that these truly are important things to learn.[7]

Model, acknowledge, and celebrate the effort in the pursuit of a chosen goal. Although some might debate the point, we see this guideline as reflecting a more Eastern than Western perspective. Learning is a courageous act and frequently involves risk. We do not know how well we will learn the novel task or topic before us. Because acquiring knowledge so often requires study, practice, concentration, revision, and overcoming mistakes, the traits of perseverance, endurance, and diligence are qualities essential to learning. Effort is the central component within those qualities. It is the hard work of daily school life. If motivation to learn is ever to become a child's value, that child will have to view effort in the service of learning as a natural and admirable personal trait—a matter of honor.

Thus in learning or in pursuing any chosen goal, we advocate treating children so that they realize that the way something is done is more important than the end accomplishment. Children need to know that trying hard and doing one's best are more important than the grade they receive or the score they attain. This approach benefits all children in the family because every one of them is capable of trying hard and doing his or her best, while all of them may not be capable of receiving high academic ratings. Within such a framework, all children can maintain their integrity.

To make effort and diligence traits that children accept and cherish also means altering the way things are commonly acknowledged in our culture. Consider, for example, two children who achieve the same level of excellence on a science project, even though one child worked much harder and much longer than the other child to accomplish this feat. Which of the two children would receive more praise from the general public? Would not the child who worked less be seen as more talented and capable? And would not the child who worked longer be seen as a good student but also be more prone to be labeled as a plodder and that worst of all damnations of faint praise, the proverbial overachiever? We think so.

Place this example in the sphere of adolescence, under the scrutiny of peers, and the effects can be devastating.[8] Whether it is a test, a project, or a simple homework assignment, to the quick and competent go the acclaims of giftedness and ability; to those who fall short of the mark and who try very hard and very long come the judgments of slow, mediocre, and at best, a hard worker, which in many adolescent peer groups translates as a fool.

The task then for parents is to make the processes of learning—such as studying, doing homework, and paying attention—virtues. Over 90 percent of learning is process. Only a few percent is performance—taking tests, participating in competitions, and publicly displaying academic work. When we acknowledge effort to learn as valued and important, our children can see the act of learning as a way to gain self-esteem and develop personal pride. This will make effort a well-developed personal trait that can be called upon as needed—much like well-developed physical strength—without leading to undue anxiety and exhaustion.

Long-distance running in the United States offers a fine analogy for this approach. Whether it is a marathon or a six-kilometer run, most of the participants see winning the race as unimportant relative to doing their personal best and enjoying the exhilaration of comradeship, fitness, and the esthetics of mind and body in motion on nature's path. The *process* of running itself is valued with each individual's sense of pride dependent, not upon winning or crossing the finish line faster than someone else, but upon participating and staying the course.

As with the previous guideline, we begin with ourselves as parents who model for our children what we want to develop within them. In most cases, if the manner is not traumatic (and there are exceptions to this), it is very good for our children to see us work hard and struggle for the things we value. If we can do so gracefully, so much the better. Classic films abound with this image: Spencer Tracy in *Captains Courageous*, Henry Fonda in *The Grapes of Wrath*, James Stewart in *It's a Wonderful Life*, Paul Winfield in *Sounder*, Claudia McNeil in *A Raisin in the Sun*, and Sally Field in *Norma Rae*.

In terms of how we treat our children, we want to acknowledge their effort, perseverance, and diligence as the occasion warrants. This can range from a simple "I like the way you try" to a detailed comment about their preparation, commitment, and painstaking endurance. Another area that provides opportunity is how we coach our children through some task such as mowing the lawn, cleaning up in the kitchen, or finishing a school project. The standards we set for completion and a job well done will tell our children how much we care about effort and diligence. For example, "I'd rather you take your time and do it well" leans toward diligence, while "just get the job done" leans away.

Giving attributes to effort for consequences is another powerful way to influence our children to make effort a valued and useful resource for learning. An attribute is a cause we give for a consequence someone has experienced. Someone gets promoted; that is a consequence. We say it is *because* they were qualified, intelligent, and diligent. Those are three attributes. Children receive consequences on a daily basis at school: grades, scores, and teacher comments. When they show us or tell us about their successful consequences, we can attribute some of the causes to effort when we believe this to be true. For example, "That is a very high score. I know how hard you studied. I'm glad to see your perseverance helped you" or "What an excellent comment your teacher made on your paper! Your extra library work made a difference. Congratulations." Children have many reasons they can believe for why they do well in school. Luck, ability, help from others, and easy assignments are a few of the many possibilities. Yet where effort has contributed to their accomplishment, they should know this. It will generally help them to feel some degree of pride and to realize they have a resource they can be confident is usually available to them.

But what if the consequence is negative, such as a low grade or a poor score? This should be approached as a problem to solve in which more effort may be a possible solution. If we have good reasons to believe that some form of greater effort (studying, practicing, rewriting) will improve our children's learning, it is wise for them to know this. It emphasizes their power and responsibility in learning and can give them real hope for future performance when similar tasks will be undertaken. (We will say much more about low grades in general in the next chapter.)

To respect a student who struggles to learn means to value the quality of persistence above achievement, to see the "hard road" as a means to refine and enhance the self. To anchor diligence within the family value system means to consider each child's merits individually, not to compare children, and certainly not to compare them on the basis of achievement. Each child differs in ability, and it is each one's personal improvement that matters most. These gains depend on each child's effort.

This also means paying more attention as parents to the effort component on the report card and taking personal responsibility to nurture and support our children's perseverance as they do their schoolwork. This means we plan with them to remove distractions and guarantee there is time available to study. We hold ourselves accountable for a share of how well our children are able to persist in learning tasks in the eyes of their teachers. It also means emphasizing the *whole* child's development in a manner that means even good grades do not excuse issues of effort, character, and citizenship.[9]

We also suggest that teachers adopt such approaches regarding effort within the classroom. This means that students can realize from the teacher's actions that doing their best is more important than the grades they receive, that when it comes to effort everyone can excel and have integrity. Teachers can encourage such beliefs by acknowledging perseverance, endurance, and diligence both verbally and in written comments on exams and assignments. This allows students to know, especially when mistakes are made and progress is slow, that continuing to try—whether it be a matter of study, practice, or preparation—is a means to preserve their dignity. For example, students who studied hard and still scored poorly on a test would remain respected by their teachers and peers.

Competition, social comparison, and grouping by ability are *not* emphasized in classroom practices. When these means of instruction are absolutely necessary, they are used with great care not to intimidate or embarrass students. Teachers who want to develop persistence as a value among their students use cooperative learning with groups of children at different skill levels, comments directed to the task of learning and ways to improve, and problem solving with children to encourage harmony. They also encourage students to do things the children themselves can control, such as obtain assistance, be prepared, and complete assignments.

Effort is worth celebrating. It has a wonderful paradoxical effect. When it is more valued than accomplishment, it means that the children's role in the classroom is not to perform better than their peers, or to avoid looking incompetent, but to strive to learn. In turn, this reduces the pressure of achievement and the fear of failure, letting the children fully embrace learning, which is the most enjoyable and best way to learn. In the long run, this kind of involvement leads to the highest achievement.[10] By placing effort above achievement in value, a teacher gets more achievement from more students than she or he would get otherwise, with the added benefit of an environment of hope and integrity for everyone.

Consistently offer a sincere expectancy that your child can learn effectively. In order to learn, children must believe that they can learn. We, as parents, are the most important adults in the lives of our children. Whatever we say or do regarding their ability to learn will have a major impact on their self-confidence as learners. Therefore, parents make a most unfortunate mistake when they negatively label their children as *dumb* or *lazy*. At the very worst, such identification dooms a child to a self-fulfilling prophecy; at the very least, it provides an easy excuse which everyone is powerless to counter. What does a parent do with a lazy child? Having noted this concern, let's move on to the positive aspects of this guideline.

When our children do well in learning at home or in school, we can show a confident joy in their accomplishments, sharing our spontaneous feelings along with a continued faith in their abilities. The attitude projected is a sincerely happy "Yes, you did; and yes, you can; and yes, you will!"

Probably the real moment of truth for parental expectancies comes when children are having or have had difficulties learning. First, patience and calmness are excellent emotions to accompany any expression of our faith in helping them to redeem the situation.

Second, the rule of thumb for the help we give is "just enough"—no more, no less, because limited assistance will enable our children to retain credit for resolving the difficulty and build their self-confidence for other trials later. In manner and form, this is similar to how most parents help toddlers learn to walk. We see how able and ready they are to walk, and then we give them just enough support—at first two hands, then one hand, and, finally, no hands when they seem capable of going it alone. We might use the same sort of approach to help children solve a frustrating arithmetic problem. We listen to understand what is confusing them. We try to figure out how ready they are to carry out the mathematical steps necessary. Then we give them enough information to get them going and support them with suggestions as needed. We don't completely do the problem for them any more than a parent would unnecessarily carry a child who was capable of walking with a little help. Even though we may know the entire route to understanding, we realize that in learning, as in life, when children believe that they are most responsible for forging ahead through difficulty, they become more confident and self-reliant.

Third, no matter what the learning difficulty, it is best to see it as a problem to be solved. This reduces frustration and blame because such a framework creates some emotional distance for everyone and implies by its very nature that there is a solution. This shows faith in the children as learners and offers a structure to build a reasonable plan in which we can cooperate with our children and the teacher to find ways to effectively continue learning.

Another critical area that reveals our expectancy for our children as learners is how we handle their mistakes in learning. To enjoy learning, children must be allowed to make mistakes without punitive consequences. If children are to learn from their mistakes, they cannot be frightened to make them. Helping them see their mistakes as clues to the best that they know at the moment is encouraging as well as realistic.[11] Treating our children's errors as information about what they still have to learn shows faith that they can learn and helps them to find personal use in errors rather than self-abuse. For example, if a child said that Henry Ford invented the light bulb, we would have a clue that the child knows that Ford was an inventor, but has some confusion about what he invented. The next step is to help the child remember or clarify his or her thinking. Dwelling on the error does little good. This is true at every level of learning.

Our expectancy for our children to learn is also shown in the opportunities we provide for them. The range of these opportunities is immense and is to some extent limited by such factors as time, money, and geography. The rule of thumb is, "If they show an interest, extend it."[12] For example, for a child who loves to read, a visit to the library should be appealing; for a child who loves science, a microscope would be a welcome gift.

We suggest teachers take a similar path to the treatment of learning difficulties and mistakes just outlined. We also want to encourage teachers to use more frequently diagnostic forms of evaluation, which are geared to determine whether or not the student has mastered what is to be learned and what, if anything, the student can do to improve.[13] To the extent that the teaching process allows students to answer questions, give opinions, and participate in classroom discussions, it is important that *all* students receive an equal opportunity to do so on meaningful tasks.[14] This, in addition to honest feedback on schoolwork, concretely lets students know that the teacher cares about their participation and expects them to learn.

Because low-achieving students often receive lower expectations from teachers, they are more likely to be treated in ways that further reduce their motivation to learn.[15] For example, teachers have been observed to wait less time for low-achieving students to answer questions than for high-achieving students. The following list offers a series of actions for teachers to consider to maintain the motivation of low-achieving students:[16]

1. Encourage them when they initiate comments.
2. Use cues and probes to help them turn incorrect answers into more accurate responses.
3. Ask for more elaboration when their answers are marginal.
4. Call on them to participate in class as much as any of the rest of the students.
5. Avoid criticizing them when their answers are wrong and when they fail to respond.
6. Avoid placing them in low-ability groups that are publicly known to the rest of the class.
7. Allow them opportunities to select study topics, evaluate their own work, and make important decisions in classroom affairs.
8. Continue to challenge them academically.

Not giving up on children is as important for teachers as it is for parents. And without a doubt, each of us needs the other's support to remain determined in our efforts.

   Help your child to structure appropriate study habits. We believe the most important aspect of study habits to be the understanding that when the school day is done, academic work and learning hold a priority that is second only to family or religious necessity. Family obligations and emergencies such as caring for a younger sibling or a sick parent might at times take precedence over homework or study, but otherwise schoolwork is the first responsibility of the child. Establishing this priority as a routine or fact of home life will greatly aid in overcoming the many distractions and attractive options that can prevent a child's involvement in academic learning.

To evaluate any activity that competes for the child's time after school, the central question is "How much will it interfere with his or her schoolwork?" When parental support is needed, such a question may pertain to parents' activities as well.

By setting a specific time or order—after supper, for example—to be used to begin studying, the child can more easily adjust other goals to fit this schedule. This makes starting schoolwork easier because other expectations or needs are always considered relative to, rather than in competition with, studying. In general, the child will benefit from doing schoolwork in an area of the home that is private and free from distraction.

To our way of thinking, study habits resemble habits of cleanliness or physical exercise; they are automatic parts of daily lives that contribute to a healthy life. In this case, it is the life of a lifelong learner who realizes that studying is not only a means to prosper but also a necessity to survive today.

When possible, the teacher should provide clear guidelines for studying and homework. These may include a rationale regarding the merits of the work, labor-saving methods, techniques to aid memory and transfer, and whatever else might make learning more rewarding in both its effort and its result. More specific ideas regarding homework will be discussed in the next chapter.

Be involved in your child's school throughout all the years of formal education. According to a special report by the National Committee for Citizens in Education, the evidence is beyond dispute: Parent involvement improves student achievement.[17] It improves positive attitudes toward school and helps motivate children to succeed. The benefits are not confined to early childhood or the elementary level; there are strong effects from parent involvement continuously throughout high school.

Our review of the research indicates that there is no one best way to be involved as a parent; parents can be involved in a variety of roles over time. The form of parental involvement does not seem to be as crucial as that it is reasonably well planned, comprehensive, and longlasting. This involvement can take three forms. The first is parent as educator to the child. This can involve the home setting where there is a positive learning environment, including supportive attitudes toward education and high expectations for success, or it can involve parents carrying out teaching activities and methods that support what occurs in the classroom, such as rewards for improved performance.[18]

The second form of parent involvement is when the parent becomes part of a program in the school, such as a tutor to his or her own child. The third form of parent involvement is as a community member supporting the school by serving on school committees and volunteering to work at school functions.

In all of these forms of involvement, two things are probably apparent to children and account to some extent for the positive influence on their motivation to learn. The first is that they readily see that their parents believe education is important. The second is that there is a formal or informal unity between the school and their parents. This integration of family with school creates a more powerful and consistent message echoed at home and reverberated in the classroom: "Learning is in your best interest and we are all here to help you accomplish it."

As parents, being involved helps us to know the teachers, be aware of the curriculum, and understand the complexities of a modern school. Through our support we become more knowledgeable and more motivated to influence more capably our children's motivation to learn.

The teacher's part in this process is to see the parent as the most important teacher in the student's life and as a partner who can powerfully and cooperatively assist in helping the student to learn. Various kinds of specific participation should be established with this attitude. It is both common sense and a profound reality that with each other's effort and trust, the student, the parent, and the teacher can gain the most, most easily.

Help your child to develop an identity as a Learner. We offer this last guideline as a way of symbolizing and supporting all of the previous guidelines. Identity is a powerful motivational force. We all do many things because we literally tell ourselves who we are and what we expect from ourselves: "I am a *parent* and it is important for me to be the one to help my child with this problem." "I'll go because I am her *friend* and she needs me now." To identify oneself as a *learner* can automatically cue a framework of attitudes, expectancies, and attributes that benefit motivation to learn. Teaching such an identity to our child can also help each of us to remember the essential components of these guidelines. This will help us as a family to develop attitudes and behavior toward learning that are mutually consistent and therefore effective in developing motivation to learn.

We also encourage the identity as a learner because we like the way the word sounds and what it implies, especially in contrast to today's popular label of *winner*. For each winner there are many losers. For each learner there can be many fellow learners. *Winner* points to the top, above the others. *Learner* points to the horizon, to sharing the view. Ultimately, what does our society most need for our young people to strive to become? The best of our knowledge and experience tells us that the choice is an important one. We offer a role any young person can take—a learner—a daughter, a son, a student who:

1. values the way something is done more than the end accomplishment
2. realizes that effort is the constant companion of personal excellence
3. knows mistakes are a natural and instructive part of learning
4. determines and holds himself or herself responsible for most of what is learned
5. seeks to make the process of learning as pleasurable as the result
6. cherishes knowledge and competence above grades

We realize that these traits are as much values as they are research-based findings. But that is the way of motivation to learn.

It is eventually as much a learned trait as it is an inherited tendency. As adults, we can make conscious decisions to influence our children to be motivated by a wide array of values. While we teach our children how to approach learning, we also teach them how to approach life. The future of our society is a rolling echo of these lessons. What kind of adults would the embodiment of these traits by children eventually create? That is an essential question for us today. If you respect and desire what you imagine them to be, we invite you to join such a vision and its responsibility.

Chapter 4

—8—

Grades, Homework, and Television: Thorny Concerns

People pay attention to what they measure.

—Elliot Eisner

Grades

ALTHOUGH MANY PEOPLE might wish it were not so, grades are the yardstick of learning that most people pay attention to. Parents brag about the grade-point averages of their children as hunters might bellow about the best of their trophies: "He pulled a 4.0 this semester and that's including calculus!" Others see them as the harbinger of disaster: "Something's wrong. She dropped below a 3.5. We'd better have a talk with her before it's too late." Students open their report cards with the sweaty fingers of an explosives expert dismantling a live grenade. Watch any group of students as they react to the report cards they have just received. Some smile, some cry, but all are very serious. In a few moments their gasps of exaltation and exasperation begin to fill the air. "I don't believe it!!! An A in biology. My parents are going to flip out." Another student responds, "Yeah, so are mine. When they see these grades, I'm grounded until the twenty-first century."

Is something amiss here? Yes. Grades are important. They are the teacher's concise documentation of learning. They are the number one criterion for admission into most universities. A severe drop in them can be an indicator of emotional problems or substance abuse.[1] The problem is that grades have become *too impor-*

tant. It is not our intention to encourage the abolishment of grades but we do say that for too many parents and for the culture at large the obsessive emphasis on grades as the true reflection of learning has reached a point of diminishing returns.[2] In some communities of this country, grades are regarded with awe akin to idolatry. Parents and college admissions officers openly worship high grade-point averages. Ask any high school senior who wants to go to a "better" university. It is disturbing to hear a young person say, "I could do anything I wanted to as long as I got good grades."

Grades have become too big a carrot in too many schools and families. From a motivational standpoint, grades are most helpful to the enjoyment of learning when they are seen as indicators of the progress and quality of learning. Grades are most oppressive when they are seen as the reason for learning.[3] Even B. F. Skinner, an orthodox advocate of external rewards, opposes grades because, as they are traditionally used, they constantly threaten and coerce students.[4] For students, school life is too often a tense, endless cycle of strife where the object is not the acquisition of learning or even of good grades, but the avoidance of bad grades.

This puts parents and teachers in a difficult quandary. We know grades are important. We know they will, to a serious extent, influence the opportunities our children receive. We also know that by emphasizing grades, we can undermine the satisfaction and meaning that learning has to offer. So how do we help our children to realize we expect them to do well in school without making grades too important or too trivial? We can begin by giving grades the reality they deserve.

As parents, we must remember and help our children to understand that *a grade is information about the progress and quality of their learning that is, at best, imprecise.* It is important because it is one of the few ways that teachers can communicate about how well students are learning. A grade doesn't tell very much about what they actually know or how effectively they could use what they are learning, but it does indicate, especially on report cards, the teacher's evaluation of this learning. We care about grades because we care about our children's learning.

A second step is to *make our expectations for our children's grades clear and reasonable.* In general, our children will tend to expect of themselves what we expect of them regarding the quality of their learning. If we expect too much of them, beyond what their best effort and ability can attain, they will likely feel frustrated, disappointed, and distressed. If we expect too little of them, we can needlessly limit their self-esteem, inspiration, and potential. So we want to consider carefully the message we send them about our expectations for the quality of their learning. By giving them a standard to strive for that is within their reach, we increase the possibilities that they will feel satisfaction with themselves upon achievement, pride in their accomplishment, growing confidence, and a self-fulfilling prophecy that they are capable learners.

Thus if we had children in a school where we thought they were capable of excellent learning, we would expect mostly A's on their report cards. Notice we said *mostly* A's, not all A's. There are good reasons for this distinction. Even the most talented students are not highly talented in all subjects. To do excellent work in a good school with reasonable standards takes demanding effort and concentration. As with shooting foul shots in basketball, the best players are going to miss at least a few times. Also, students who love what they are learning develop preferences. They might want to spend more time and creativity on their favorite subjects. More power to them! It's okay for great physicists to be fair writers and for great writers to be mediocre physicists.

Another important consideration regarding grades is how we respond to them. *When our children meet or surpass a standard of learning that we believe they are capable of, and their grades reflect this, we are wise to emphasize the attributes that led to such grades.* We can comment on the ability, effort, planning, studying, creativity, writing skills, and all the other things that good grades reflect. This puts grades in their rightful place as mirrors and focuses on the substance that learning really is. This is beneficial because it helps our children learn their capabilities, which are what they will need and use in their jobs. Such an awareness of knowledge, skill, and determination builds pride and confidence in people. We can establish such positive self-awareness in our children by responding to their report cards and grades with comments like "Oh, I see you received an A in chemistry. That's great. I'm really happy to see your talent resulting in excellent work." "A B in Spanish. That's an improvement since your last marking. Nice to see all that hard work making a difference!" In life, it is the hard work and talent that make a difference, not some grade in a high school class. Young people need to know about their capacity for hard work and about their talents. Grades just help us to point out these assets to them. In this way, grades serve one of their most useful purposes.

When our children's grades do not reflect a standard of learning that we believe they are capable of, we treat this as diagnostic information. Something is wrong. This is what low grades tell us. It is a time for compassion, problem solving, and encouragement. One of our first responses needs to be empathy for what our children may be feeling; we need to share our realizations of their possible disappointment, frustration, or anger. If they have tried very hard or done their best, then our acknowledgment of such perseverance, at this time, can support their dignity and sense of pride: "I know you did your best and that's what counts the most." It is also important to realize that such a statement is more than an empty cliché and reflects our parental commitment to help solve the problem and to remain an encouraging force in our children's efforts.

We want to find out from our children's perspective what they think the problem might be. It is best for their own motivation to participate in finding and planning the solution. This gives them a sense of self-determination, responsibility, and a real investment in the outcome of this process. It also teaches them to learn how to help themselves. If it is necessary to bring the teacher into the resolution of the difficulty, treat this person as you would a knowledgeable and concerned consultant. We regret that both the research and our clinical experience strongly indicate that when people are unsuccessful in sports, work, or learning, they are likely to blame external causes rather than search within their own behavior for possible answers.[5] Teachers too often fall prey to this inclination. Unquestionably, a teacher, parents, and student working cooperatively to solve a learning problem will be far more motivated and far more successful than the same group approaching the problem in mistrustful conflict. (More suggestions for problem solving and encouragement are contained in Part Two.)

The role of the teacher is critical when it comes to grades

because it is the teacher who most often sets the standards and criteria for grades, manages the evaluations, and assigns grades. Grading is a very complex process. Within the field of education there are many unresolved standing arguments about the best ways to evaluate and grade students.[6] In general, we oppose grading on a curve and norm-referenced grading.[7] Both of these approaches limit student performance to fixed percentages so that there *must always be students who do below-average work.* Thus a significant number of students (sometimes up to 50 percent) are automatically denied acknowledgment of successful performance in learning, no matter how hard they try. To imagine how unfair these evaluative standards potentially can be, consider this scenario. A teacher used strictly the normal curve to grade a twenty-word spelling test for twenty-five students; due to a combination of fine ability and intense effort, twelve students had twenty words spelled correctly, one had nineteen words spelled correctly, and twelve had eighteen words spelled correctly. The students who spelled eighteen words correctly were considered below average on that particular test and eligible for no more than a C grade, even though they had spelled 90 percent of the words correctly.

This situation doesn't happen very often, and most teachers would be wise enough to throw out the normal curve evaluation if it did. But it does illustrate how irrational, arbitrary, and harmful to motivation norm-referenced standards of evaluation can be in a classroom. Those who use this system destine half their students to think they lack success in learning. Because a feeling of competence is so necessary to develop motivation to learn within people, these "below-average" students are likely to lose their desire to learn.

We favor the fixed standard method of grading in which teachers assign levels of performance or criteria of competence that qualitatively distinguish what is excellent to inadequate learning in a given subject.[8] These distinctions can include learning as exhibited on tests, papers, projects, and classroom participation. The advantage of this system is that students understand what they must do to indicate the quality of their learning and receive the grade appropriate to that quality. This puts the determination of grades more into students' hands and helps them to plan and persevere for the standards they wish to meet. In this manner, grades are more informational than coercive.

Employing this criteria-referenced system of grading, the teacher in the preceding example would have told the students in advance how many words spelled correctly would result in a particular grade on the test. With standards set so that A = 19-20 correct, B = 17-18 correct, and C = 15-16 correct, the scores reported earlier would have resulted in thirteen students receiving A's and twelve receiving B's. None of the students would be forced to see themselves as below average, and all of the students could consider themselves good spellers.

The key to making grades a more intrinsically motivating component in learning is to make them more informational than controlling. When teachers have valid methods to assess learning and can communicate these methods and their criteria precisely to students, the students know grades are more likely to be reasonable and fair reflections of what they have learned.

Part of the problem with evaluation and grades is the enormous amount of time it can take to construct or check a valid test or other measure of learning competence. Parents concerned about grades need to understand this. To make up a good fair test means analyzing all the important ideas and skills that have been taught, selecting the most important among them, and designing tasks that allow students to reveal what they should have learned about these essentials. In many ways it is very much like creating an original puzzle and then making sure someone can follow it. This takes time. We offer the following suggestions with a healthy respect for the exhaustive constraints of testing and evaluation. Retesting, arranging contracts, and giving extra assignments are possible ways to allow students to improve their learning, show evidence for it, and thereby improve their grades. *Retesting* means that a different test covering the same material must be available or constructed. *Contracts* mean a specific grade is offered for required levels of accomplishment on various tasks. *Extra assignments* mean that the students can demonstrate increased learning by doing another project or writing another paper. For all three of these possibilities, there must be time available to both the teacher and the students to do the extra work. In each of these instances, students can readily see how perseverance can contribute to their learning. However, if teachers use any of these methods, they should explain to students early in the course how they will be used so all students have a chance to consider these options.

We agree with Thomas Good and Jere Brophy that every teacher who must use grades should set standards that allow every student to obtain at least a grade of C, or whatever grade indicates *satisfactory* learning.[9] This does not mean that every student will achieve at least a C, but it does mean that the teacher has arranged the conditions of learning and evaluation so that students who persevere can succeed. Learning does not have to be excellent to be enjoyable, but to be motivating, it does have to move along, showing progress and improvement that is convincing.

Homework

Listen to it. The word has a bad sound. Homework. You've got homework. *Home* sounds nice. But *work* sounds bad. Why would we ever want to put something bad into someplace nice? And that is one of the biggest mistakes we ever made with homework—its name. We should have called it homelearning or, better yet, homeplay. Or maybe a rollicking-good-time-with-books. No one likes homework. Did you? Did we? Maybe once or twice. But not so much that we would readily admit to it when we were adolescents. It's nerdy, un-American, and weird to like homework.

Yet the life of a learner is the life of homework. Scientists, engineers, researchers, professors, teachers, mechanics, and actors continuously read, write, solve problems, and compute. In the information age, in the twenty-first century, in a technologically dominated world, life and work will be more and more made up of what today passes as the guts of most academic assignments. Thus the attitude we suggest to parents is to encourage our children to see homework as a matter-of-fact and valued part of their lives—forever.

One way of looking at homework is to compare it to personal grooming. It is something we all need to do, so let us do it well. How to make it satisfying and motivating is the larger question. To answer this, we must move away from the cosmetic to the substantial. We have previously established our rationale for diligence as a valued trait among children. Diligence greatly supports pleasurable involvement in homework as physical fitness greatly supports pleasurable involvement in athletics. Tennis and basketball are wonderful, enjoyable sports, but they will be painful and short lived for those lacking physical conditioning. Thoughtful homework can provide real learning, but it will have little chance to do so if the student sees effort as a constant trial and tribulation.

Yet diligence is not enough. The Japanese say, "If you do not understand it, read it 100 times, and you will understand it."[10] We admire the virtue of such persistence, but realize how extreme such an attitude would be in our own culture. Americans seek more balance between effort and outcome.

One way to make homework less oppressive is to help ourselves and our children to realize that work is not necessarily more important than play and that play is not necessarily more enjoyable than work. When people can act with their full abilities in situations that are challenging and allow further growth, they find them worthwhile and enjoyable.[11] Sports is a good example. The most closely contested games are the most absorbing and enjoyable for participants and spectators alike. A parallel situation in work would be a plumber solving a challenging problem that demands the best of his or her skills and experience. Is not one of the most enjoyable aspects of teaching reaching challenging students and making a difference with skills and effort?

This points to one of the paradoxes of motivation. When something becomes easy, it often loses its motivating influence. Easy work, easy learning, and, oddly enough, easy play, are fertile ground for boredom, indifference, and cynicism. As parents, by helping our children to see homework as a daily challenge, an endeavor through which their knowledge and abilities will grow, we form a context that makes "hitting the books" a desirable and empowering activity for them. By sharing with our children how our own jobs and leisure time have elements of homework that we find rewarding, we can help them to perceive homework as a natural and automatic engagement.

Teachers can make a significant difference in the quality of students' involvement in homework. Homework is the area in which teachers and parents share one of their most concrete partnerships for the benefit of children. Homework helps children to learn. In a sense, homework is the teacher's daily message to parents, saying, indirectly, "I care about these children and am helping them to prosper in learning." Teachers can help both students and parents to regard homework positively when they apply the following six points:

1. *Make the assignment directly relevant to the lesson or unit that is being conducted in the classroom.* Then there can be no misgivings about the importance of the assignment.
2. *Give assignments that are clear and that require skills and knowledge that are within the range of students' capabilities.* It is extremely frustrating to want to do homework well and to be unable to do it. Getting stuck on math problems is the classic example. Parents can sometimes help their children with homework, but, as stated earlier, *just enough* is the rule of thumb. Also, a cooperative telephone network among the students can serve as temporary assistance and be sanctioned by the teacher.
3. *Give assignments that are challenging and stimulating.* The teacher should be personally enthusiastic about them. A legitimate criterion: How would the teacher feel if he or she were asked to do the assignments?
4. *Hold students accountable for completion of assignments.* Unquestionably, this is where parents must support teachers. A breach in the parent-teacher partnership over this issue is deadly to student motivation.[12]
5. *Comment on completed assignments, orally or in writing.* Although this is vastly time-consuming, it is a powerful motivational influence for students because it can provide corrective feedback, acknowledge positive qualities in student work, exhibit caring and attention frequently unavailable in the classroom, and testify to the importance of the work.
6. *Brief parents on your system of handling homework.* Make sure they know the amount of homework you typically assign, its function, the frequency of assignment, and your expectations or possible requests for parental support, involvement, and cooperation. This can often be accomplished in a letter that

parents are requested to read and sign at the beginning of the school year.

Television

If Karl Marx were to wander among the homes of America, he would probably change his famous dictum to "Television is the opiate of the masses." Children between the ages of six and eleven watch, on the average, twenty-seven hours of television a week, the equivalent of two months a year.[13]

Television is not inherently bad. It has some redeeming value. We can see history in the making, science and medicine as they are practiced, and join in the varied splendor of the human arts. However, television is severely polluted. Like contaminated water, it can appear seemingly harmless and inviting. It is only much later that the illness is evident. TV viewing is the most significant predictor of obesity in children, with excess weight increasing 1 percent for each hour of TV watched per week.[14] By the time the average child graduates from high school, he or she will have watched 18,000 murders, been exposed to an hourly average of more than 13 examples of explicitly sexual behavior, and have viewed 24,000 beer and wine commercials.[15]

The mind processes information. That is a fact. Television is information. That's also a fact. Much of the information on television is rubbish. That's a value. Children who indiscriminately watch television continuously process rubbish. That's an opinion. Studies do show a relationship between adverse effects on the imaginative and creative abilities of children and heavy exposure to standard commercial television programming.[16] However, from a scientific perspective, it has not been demonstrated that watching vast amounts of television is a direct cause of poor school performance.

It is not the corrosive potential of television upon the mind that alone bothers us; its destructive force upon the soul also deeply disturbs us. Motivation is more spirit than thought. It is the stuff of will, determination, and endurance. Television viewing erodes such qualities because it literally replaces them. It deposes activity with passivity. It eliminates initiative with docility and displaces thoughtfulness with stupor. Children do not want to do their homework because they would rather watch television. They sloppily rush through their homework in order to watch television, which offers the opportunity for a continuous dismal pleasure without any requirement of responsibility, effort, or courage. That is why watching it will never build a child's confidence, character, or sense of justifiable pride. Television is a terrible seduction. It can turn a young person into a "couch potato" in the worst sense that this image can convey. We genuinely believe television sets should come, as cigarettes do, emblazoned with a warning about their hazards to a person's well-being. We suggest:

1. Limiting your children's television viewing to no more than ten hours weekly.[17]
2. Planning television viewing with your children and helping them to select quality programs. (Teachers can be helpful by alerting families to programs that are supportive of academic learning and relevant to current lessons.)
3. Deliberately *not* offering television viewing as a reward or incentive for homework completion because such action would make television only more desirable and contradict other measures being taken to lessen the influence of TV.
4. Replacing television viewing with an involving and productive set of activities; for example, reading, sports, exercise, games, puzzles, and, best of all, doing things together, such as making something, cooking, reading, and having *conversations.*
5. Practicing what you preach by applying standards to your own television viewing that are similar to the ones you advocate for your children.

One of the most important conclusions drawn from motivation research is that the amount of time people spend on particular tasks often reflects the strength of their motivation for the task.[18] With this reasoning, a case can be made that young Americans are more motivated to watch television than they are motivated to learn. It is estimated that of the average of six hours that students spend in school, approximately three and a half of them are spent actually engaged in learning. That is a total of seventeen and a half hours per week. In the 1981 High School and Beyond Study of more than 55,000 students, the students themselves reported that they were averaging four to five hours of homework and about twenty-eight hours of television per week.[19] That makes a total of about twenty-two hours of learning versus twenty-eight hours of watching television, not including summers and holidays. Because many students do other things while watching television, including homework, we cannot pin down the exact ratio. However, these estimates are enough to make us very concerned.

Without a doubt, too many children are more motivated to watch television than they are motivated to learn. When you think of the content of a good book compared to the superficial entertainment of the average television program, the exponential folly of this predicament is frightening—a waste of minds and the motivation of our youth. Parents can change this.

Part II

How to Support a Child's Learning and Solve Motivational Problems

INTO THE ACADEMIC LIVES of all students come times when they have to deal with failure, poor grades, boredom, fatigue, loss of determination, and tests that are downright scary. This is school life, and even the most motivated have lasting setbacks, doubts, fears, and anxieties. As parents and teachers, we know that a bad day for a child can turn into a bad week, a bad month, or a bad semester. Early adolescence, eleven to fifteen years of age, is an especially turbulent time for children and a risky time for motivation to learn and school achievement.[1]

Whenever young people have problems with motivation to learn, we as parents and teachers want to know how to help them regain their hope, how to restore their confidence, revive their determination, sustain their perseverance, and help them return to enthusiastic learning. The following pages offer discussion and explanations of practical ways to foster motivation. These methods do not work in a vacuum. They are far more likely to succeed when the suggestions for developing children's motivation to learn, outlined in Part One, are essential influences in their lives.

We begin by looking at how to establish a positive relationship between the parent and the teacher.

Chapter 5

Building a Positive
Parent-Teacher Relationship

*One man may hit the mark, another blunder; but heed not
these distinctions. Only from the alliance of the one, working
with and through the other, are great things born.*

—Antoine de Saint-Exupéry

A POSITIVE RELATIONSHIP between the school and the home is an
important contributor to students' achievements in school.[1] In fact,
the positive relationship itself is of even greater value than the sum
of simply adding good home influences to good school influences.
The interaction of influences provides an important and powerful
factor in creating an atmosphere supportive to learning.

For example, it is helpful for teachers to clearly explain
homework assignments. It is also helpful for parents to enforce
expectations for homework completion. Both are important. When
these separate efforts are combined with parents and teachers meeting together to make the reasons for homework assignments clear to
students, this cooperative effort can even more positively influence
the motivation of students to learn. This influence is powerful because of the integration of parents' and teachers' efforts and the
consistent message that is communicated to students.

Although we recognize that cooperation between teachers
and parents is extremely important in encouraging school success,
all too often parents and teachers find themselves in conflict when
problems emerge. In these situations, teachers frequently blame
home and family influences while parents blame the school.[2] Why
does this happen?

One primary reason is that many times parents and teachers have had little or no contact with one another prior to the event or incident leading to identification of a problem. Because of this lack of contact, there has been no opportunity for the building of mutual trust in a safe and secure setting—a setting in which an attitude of problem solving prevails, the best interest of the student is paramount, and communication is direct and clear.

If parents and teachers communicate only when there is a problem, the context is often set for resistance. When hearing from a teacher has only meant trouble in the past, parents may understandably be reluctant and cautious when the teacher contacts them, even though it may be for an entirely different reason. For example, parents who have heard only negative news about their child from a teacher may not be particularly enthusiastic when that teacher approaches them with a request for assistance at a school function. The parent may, in fact, refuse the request. The teacher may, in turn, interpret the refusal as apathy and may then feel justified in blaming the parent for any problems the student may have. This creates a cycle of misinterpretation and miscommunication.

Barriers to positive parent-teacher relationships are created by other cycles as well. For example, cultural factors, including racial and socioeconomic differences, can contribute to ongoing alienation when certain behaviors are misread and unfairly judged. Parents who may have experienced rejection or exclusion in school because they belong to a cultural minority may choose not to attend some school functions. They decide to stay away because of their many past negative experiences. School personnel may then interpret the absence of these parents as a sign of disinterest. Teachers may then feel justified in not continuing to reach out to the parents whom they have judged to be apathetic. As the teacher sees it, "They don't care." This in turn may cause parents to feel that their decision to keep their distance was indeed the right one. As they see it, "Why do we need more rejection?"

Other parents could have recently immigrated and may be confused or intimidated by the school. But you do not have to be from a foreign country to be wary of a school system. It is a feeling similar to that many people have going into a hospital. If you do not understand how the system works, you can find it unsettling.

When we look at those cycles of suspicion, we see that it serves no useful purpose to blame either the teacher or the parents or even to try to figure out exactly where the cycle began. Doing this is like asking two children who have been fighting, "Who started it?" You usually get nowhere and you don't look at the more important question, "Where do we go from here?"

Building Positive Relationships

Teachers and parents do not wish to communicate infrequently or focus only on problems. Time pressures, multiple responsibilities, and unspoken assumptions and expectations all contribute to everyone's putting off efforts to build a positive relationship. This is unfortunate because time spent on building such a relationship can pay off in many ways. These include:

- the establishment of mutual trust
- the expressed shared goal of the best interest of the child
- the creation of a vehicle for continued open communication
- the clarification of an attitude of collaboration in problem solving rather than of blaming

The reasons for building such a relationship are compelling. Now, how is this accomplished?

Many of the ideas suggested here take time. However, more time will be saved in the long run if initial efforts are made to establish open lines of communication. Students will benefit and problems can be dealt with much more efficiently if and when they later appear. Time spent on communication at the beginning of the school year is an investment in time saved later on. But, most important, these efforts will positively affect the students' motivation to learn.

What the Teacher Can Do

There are many ways that the teacher can open the door to building direct communication and mutual trust with parents. These include contacting parents through personal phone calls during which the teacher introduces herself and expresses her willingness to answer their questions and listen to their concerns. The calls can be very brief, but well-timed and well-intended gestures of recognition can mean a great deal, even when little time is involved.

For teachers with many students and many classes, individual phone calls may be impossible. In these cases, teachers can send a letter to parents communicating the same message. This is not as personal as a phone call, but it is far better than no communication at all. The main idea is to let parents know that you as a teacher are available and accessible to them.

Some teachers send students home with an open-ended questionnaire asking parents for information that might be helpful to the teacher. This questionnaire may ask about the student's health history, the student's study habits, special family situations, and recent events in the family, such as the birth of a child or parental illness. Such requests must be made in the context of assisting the child and must indicate that the option of not completing all items of the questionnaire is acceptable. The intent is not to pry but to gather helpful information, and it is important to communicate this purpose. This questionnaire might also request information about the parents themselves, such as particular skills or knowledge that they might have that could be used in the classroom. The question of whether parents would be willing to share their expertise with students could also be addressed (while acknowledging the busy and demanding schedules that many parents have).

Other opportunities for teachers to express their availability to parents are school open-houses, parents' nights at school, PTA or PTO meetings, and parent conferences. However, these events are usually highly structured, and it is often difficult for much personal contact and sharing of information to take place. For this reason, we recommend that additional efforts, such as those described here, be made. Please see Resources A, B, and C for gathering and sharing information with parents for conferences and developing better home-school communications.[3]

What Parents Can Do

It is not necessary to wait for the teacher to take the initiative in opening lines of communication. Parents can take the initiative and contact teachers either by phone or in writing, giving teachers any information that may be useful and expressing availability should more information be needed. Parents can also prepare for conferences with the teacher by organizing their thoughts, concerns, and supportive ideas on paper and bringing such a checklist to the conference with them. See Resource D.

It can be useful for the parent to offer assistance to the teacher and while doing this to describe personal skills and knowledge that might be useful in the classroom. For example, parents can inform teachers about any special talents (musical, artistic, athletic, linguistic) or hobbies (storytelling, pets, collections such as stamps and coins, microcomputers) and also express their willingness to help in such activities as tutoring (classroom), supervising (library and playground), and consulting (legal, technical, and mechanical). At the same time, parents can mention limitations. For example, a parent may have a work or travel schedule that makes arranging conferences with the teacher difficult. It is important for the teacher to know this so she can adjust her workday to see parents at times that accommodate their jobs and other responsibilities. People employed in the service sector, such as waitresses, landscapers, or housekeepers, may have working hours that make seeing a teacher during the school day nearly impossible. By sharing their work schedules with teachers, parents send the message that they may not be easily available but they do want to be cooperative.

Parents can help the teacher by responding to invitations to school events or requests for information or assistance, even if the response means letting the teacher know that such participation may be difficult. When teachers know why parents cannot participate, misunderstandings can be minimized.

Parents can also help by giving attendance at school events a high priority. Recognizing the importance of taking advantage of every opportunity to learn about their child's education is a crucial element for parents to successfully support the school's efforts toward providing a quality academic experience. When parents are informed, when they better understand the goals and methods of the teacher, they can work to enhance their child's educational experience.

What Parents and Teachers Can Do Together

In setting a positive context for creative problem solving, both sides need to establish open lines of communication. It is also important for parents and teachers to assume that the other is doing the best job that he or she can do. Assume that you both have the student's best interest at heart, and then clarify the expectations you have of one another. Agree to enlist each other's help when needed and acknowledge that blame is a dead-end street. Also, plan to let each other know about positive observations, such as improvement in a student's study habits or attitude toward learning. Set the stage for collaboration and cooperation, and plan to act at the earliest signs of possible trouble, without waiting for the other to take the initiative.

Start by Defining the Problem. The first step in a collaborative effort toward solving school problems is for the parent and the teacher to reach a mutually agreed-upon definition of exactly what the problem is. If a child is not participating as an involved and motivated learner, it is most helpful if parents and the teacher can see this as a shared problem that they will address together rather than as something to blame one another for. If the teacher defines the problem as the result of the child living with a single parent, being adopted, or having an alcoholic parent, there is little incentive to include parents in addressing the problem. If parents see the teacher as unfair, rigid, or prejudiced, they will be reluctant to work cooperatively.

Parents and teachers can work toward defining the problem similarly by sharing the goal of describing the situation in a way that avoids blame. What exactly is happening? What behavior or attitudes need to change for things to improve? What might be another way to look at and understand things? For example, opening statements for describing the situation might be "Let me describe what Sarah is doing and what happens as a result of it. Then we can both discuss what we think about it."

Experiment to Find the Solution. The next step is to approach possible solutions with an attitude of experimentation. "Let's try this. If it works, great. If it doesn't, we will have learned something that will help us figure out what to try next."

In this way, trying to solve the problem is not something that is seen only in terms of success or failure, but rather as an attempt to find the best path to resolve the problem together. This may involve further experimenting as needed information is gathered. Parents and teachers can be active participants in this process and can provide support and encouragement for one another as the necessary data are acquired and as a successful method of addressing the problem is achieved.

How Teachers Can Enlist the Help of Parents

It is important for the teacher to communicate: "We have a common interest. We both want to help the student." This may need to be said more than once and in different ways.

If a teacher identifies a problem, it is far more helpful to enlist a parent's help with it early on than to wait until the problem has become seemingly unmanageable.

Compare these two approaches: (1) "I've recently noticed some signs that Eric isn't concentrating in class as he used to. Have you noticed similar behavior at home? Do you have any ideas about this that can help us decide what to do?" and (2) "Eric hasn't been concentrating in class for months now. I don't know what to do with him. What do you suggest?"

The first approach assumes that the sharing of information and ideas, before the problem has grown, will be effective in addressing the problem. The second approach throws the problem at the parent and then only when things have gotten out of hand, clearly destroying any possibilities for collaboration.

Catching the potential problem as early as possible is, of course, the ideal approach to resolving it. However, this is not always possible. Teachers and parents have many demands on their time and energy, and there are times when a problem is not noticed until it is full blown.

When a problem with a student has become a serious one, parents may resist approaches for help or may become hostile or even belligerent. These behaviors often reflect their frustration and concern. If teachers can recognize that, they can offer empathy rather than argument. They can express their understanding that when we are afraid or feel impotent, we are often angry. For example, it can be helpful for the teacher to respond with a remark such as "Sometimes we reach a point where we're really fed up" or "These kids can really push us to our limits." The key is not to argue or become defensive but to find a way to agree.

Here are two other examples of how this can be done: (1) If the parent blames the school and says, "The classes are too large," the teacher might say, "That may be. That's why we need your help." (2) If the parent blames the problem on the child's friends with a comment like "It's all because of the kids she's hanging around with," the teacher may agree that peers can be influential and this might be part of the problem, and then point out that this is why the parents and the teacher need to work together.

The main point is to provide support for the parents' position while using this as the rationale for working together. Sometimes parents may claim to have given up on their child with statements like "I don't know what to do any more; I've tried everything and nothing works." At such moments, it is helpful to reply with empathic remarks—"Yes, I feel that way sometimes, but I keep on trying because I know there has to be a way. It really can help to work with someone on problems like this." Arguing changes the focus from the child's problem to disagreement between the parents and the teacher. Empathizing and offering to join forces shows that you understand what the parents are experiencing and that you even share those feelings at times.

An attitude of empathy rather than blame opens the door to exploring what has and has not worked in the past and to acknowledging efforts the parents have made, even if in their eyes those efforts have not been successful.

How Parents Can Enlist the Help of the Teacher

There are times when parents may begin to suspect that their child's lack of effort or achievement in school may stem from the teacher's incompetence or insensitivity. For example, a child who has previously performed well in a specific subject may start bringing home papers with low grades but with no comments explaining the reasons for the grades. When asked about this, the child says, "The teacher doesn't explain anything."

The parent then asks, "Have you asked the teacher for help?"

And the child answers, "Yes, and he says if I listened in class I wouldn't need help. But I do listen!"

At this point the parent feels stuck right in the middle. Questions arise: "Is it possible that my child really isn't listening in class?"

"Could it be that the teacher truly is neglecting my child's needs?"

"What do I do next?"

Parents in such situations often feel torn. They want to support their child, but they also feel it is important not to undermine the authority of the teacher. When this happens, parents can take a number of different paths. Sometimes parents choose to keep their opinion to themselves, not say anything to their child or the teacher, and hope that the school year will soon end. Other parents may go immediately to the principal, demanding redress for the apparent wrongdoing or requesting a transfer to another teacher.

We do not recommend ignoring the problem or going beyond the teacher to first address the problem. Rather, we advocate the direct approach: going to the teacher with concerns as soon as they emerge. This allows the opportunity for issues to be clarified firsthand and for all concerned to express their views of the situation to one another face to face. It is often helpful to include the student in these conferences.

Decide, before approaching the teacher, specifically what you would like to discuss. When you speak with the teacher, describe your concerns without blaming the teacher for the problem. For example, if you feel that your child is not getting enough feedback on written papers, it would be more helpful to explain this and ask for clarification than to criticize or attack the teacher.

Compare: (1) "Jenny doesn't seem to understand why she received a C on last week's paper. Can you help clarify this?" to (2) "How are students supposed to know how to improve when all they get is a letter grade?"

The first approach assumes that the teacher wants to help

and may have an explanation for what has happened. The second is critical and accusatory and is unlikely to result in cooperative problem solving.

It is important as a parent to express your willingness to work with the teacher in solving identified problems. Parents can offer support to the teacher by setting appropriate limits and consequences and by using the teacher as a consultant. The teacher can help parents establish reasonable expectations if parents request this by asking, for example, "What is a realistic amount of time I can expect my child to spend on the homework you assign?" or "What do you think might be the best way for my child to study for exams?"

It can be very helpful for a parent to tell the teacher what the teacher has done that seems to have been helpful to the student in the past. This can shed light on possible solutions for the present problem by giving the teacher an opportunity to consider what has worked and what might work again.

Summary

In summary, it is most helpful for both parents and teachers to assume that:

- both are concerned and competent people
- both are making their best efforts for the good of the student
- both have to contend with pressures and responsibilities
- both need support in their efforts toward problem solving

In addition, it is most helpful to see an identified problem as a mutual challenge shared by the parents and the teacher. More is accomplished by looking for a creative solution than by looking for someone to blame. The truth is that problems do not usually have one simple identifiable cause. They are often the result of a set of circumstances or events in the school setting, combined with other factors such as the students' developmental transitions and changes at home. For example, an adolescent boy in the throes of puberty, who has not eaten for twenty-four hours and is having problems with inconsistent curfew limits set at home, comes to school feeling very hostile. The teacher asks him to work out a tricky math problem at the chalkboard. He refuses. She asks him to do the same problem at his desk. He still refuses. In fact, he refuses to do any work that day in that class. What should the teacher do? Is this a motivational problem? A nutritional problem? A developmental problem? Or a family problem? All of the aspects of a situation need to be examined in order to arrive at a workable solution. Little can be achieved if a parent says the problem is that "the teacher doesn't understand my child" or if the teacher says that "that parent is inconsistent." Both need to recognize the complexity of most problems and to work together toward effective problem solving. Parents have information that teachers need to know, and teachers have information that parents need to know. Both have a responsibility to initiate communication so that they can share this information. Waiting for the other to make the first move delays this and allows problems to escalate.

Chapter 6

Fostering Success in Learning

Gumption: shrewd practical common sense especially as actively applied to the problems of life.

—Webster's Ninth New Collegiate Dictionary

GUMPTION IS THE GUARDIAN ANGEL of motivation to learn. It is a handy first-aid kit for the bruises left by a poor grade. It is Alfred E. Newman signing off, "What, me worry?" on a low SAT score. It is the ghostbuster in the haunted house of final-exam week. It is probably more attitude than action. Its essence is the realization by parent and child that in learning, both success and failure are relative and impermanent. Life does go on, from the first grade to the rest of our lives. You do your best.

Students rarely like a subject in which they are unsuccessful. Competent progress in learning is one of the surest ways to sustain a positive attitude toward a subject.[1] When students initially fail on a reasonable learning task and believe their effort was sufficient, they usually feel some combination of confusion, frustration, and discouragement. If they continue to maintain what they believe to be sufficient effort on the learning task and cannot improve to a level they accept as satisfactory, the motivational consequences can range from indifference to hopelessness.[2]

Lack of success is subjective—a grade of B for one student may be a victory and for another a defeat—so we define it for our purposes as any evaluation of learning that students perceive as unsatisfactory and as interfering with their motivation to learn. They are having difficulty maintaining their effort to learn, and their desire to know about a particular subject is in a state of decline. Evaluations of learning include exam scores, grades, the teacher's remarks, and anything that reflects a judgment of their learning.

For parents helping a child to deal with a lack of success, we suggest the following steps:

1. Appraise the seriousness of the situation. Young people are very emotional, but they are also very resilient. In some cases time, listening, and patience will accommodate the situation. For example, a child is complaining about a low test score. But the test was really a short quiz, and the low score will have only a small impact on the child's overall evaluation. The student is feeling temporarily frustrated and is blowing off steam. By listening, the parent shows care and reasonable concern. By being patient and *not* jumping in with solutions, agreement, or blame, the situation eventually reveals itself for what it is—a child's small burst of frustration. However, if the situation appears to be serious, continue to consider the following actions.

2. Be compassionate. Children need to know we are on their side. We estimate, without being too dogmatic, what we think their feelings and concerns might be, letting them know we are available to listen and to help. "I imagine you're probably feeling discouraged right now. Want to talk about it? There are probably some ways to make this situation better. Let's look at it together." This example is meant to reveal more the essence of this approach than to dictate exact wording, which would vary according to the situation and the culture. The parent may need to spend a good deal of time listening before taking step three.

3. Emphasize the positive side of the situation. Gumption starts here. This is not the only place or the final time to do it, but now we are helping our children to find what they can learn from this experience. We involve our children in *collaborative effort.* We are detectives together looking for clues to improve the situation. Our efforts add integrity to our actions. Our mistakes give us more information and show that we need to learn more.

4. Decide what the problem is. What causes led to the unsatisfactory evaluation? Enlist the children's opinions. Ask for examples. How much difference would more effort make? How much difference would a better strategy for learning make? By when must it be solved? When is the next chance to resolve the problem? Are retesting, contracts, or other assignments a possibility? Should the teacher be consulted? If so, this is the point at which to involve the teacher in the rest of this process.

   5. Consider and select solutions. Questions like "What are some of the different *ways* that we might solve this problem?" are helpful as a starting point. Be flexible. Everyone's opinion is valuable. Use brainstorming to generate possible solutions. In the beginning, all ideas are valid. After the ideas have been exhausted is the time to evaluate them for effectiveness. When problems are complicated and involved, the following three strategies may be beneficial:

- *Means-ends analysis:* The problem is divided into a number of subproblems and then a means of solving each is worked out. For example, students want to improve the quality of their next fifteen-page term paper. Working with them, we decide to break this task into several subproblems such as selecting a topic, locating sources of information, reading and organizing the information, and making an outline. Depending on the situation, the students can then create a plan to accomplish each of these tasks.
- *Working backward:* Some problems are best considered by looking first at the goal and moving back from it to see the order and timing of what needs to be done to solve them. Let's say the students want to improve their scores on the next exam and believe they need more time to read, organize notes, and study. They might begin by looking at the date of this exam, deciding they need at least three hours to study their notes the day before the exam, and realizing they must have their notes fully organized two days before the exam and their reading completed as well, which means. . . .
- *Giving reasons for each step of a solution:*[3] When people explain why each step of a solution is necessary, it clarifies it for everyone. This *verbalization* acts as an open form of analysis and often promotes clearer steps for other parts of the solution.

For example, "If I want to do a better job on my English homework, I need to check my punctuation before I hand it in because that's where most of my mistakes were last time, when I
handed in the paper without checking its punctuation. I guess I
better check the spelling, too, because. . . ."

6. Make a plan and follow it. The solutions have been selected. When there is more than one, it helps to write them down
and organize them into some order of priority. If this doesn't seem
necessary, the adults working with the students should at least check
for understanding to make sure the plan is clear. This means asking
the students to repeat what they are going to do. For example, a
student plans to improve his learning as reflected by higher quiz
scores by the first of the month. He will budget more time to study
and if this does not work, he will tell his parents and investigate
getting a tutor: "I understand that I will budget extra time to improve. If I run into too many problems and my quiz scores don't get
better by the first of the month, I'll let you know and we'll look into
the possibility of getting a tutor to help me." Such clarity helps to
avoid disagreements and confusion.

While students carry out the plan, they should monitor how
the plan is being followed and working out. They can do this with a
checklist, an outline, a calendar of set dates, or after appropriate
points of evaluation. Sometimes adults (parents and/or teachers)
should assess the plan too. In the preceding example about quiz
scores, adults might meet with the student after each quiz to see how
things are coming along. Every plan should be open to necessary
changes.

7. Encourage! Encourage! Encourage! Once the plan is initiated, the adults involved need to show the students (1) that no
matter how the plan works out they are respected as people, (2) that
we trust and believe in their effort to improve, and (3) that we
believe they *can* do it.[4] We discuss specific ways to be encouraging
in detail later in this chapter. Students can help to encourage themselves by realizing that they have contributed to their own improvement and reminding themselves that they are doing their best, that
the goal is within reach, and that people have faith in them no

matter what the outcome. At the very least, they will learn some-thing and life will go on.

   8. Evaluate the results. Once the plan or solution has been completed, it is time to see how well things turned out. To what extent has the goal been accomplished? Are the students satisfied with the results? What has been learned? When adults are involved, this evaluation should take the form of a collaborative dialogue. No matter what, students should feel affirmed that they have tried hard and followed through on their plan.

   For steps 4, 5, 6, and 8, diplomacy and sensitivity on the part of adults are essential. We need to temper being judgmental and, even when the students' responses appear to be out of sync with real-ity, it is best to explore these with them without assigning blame. For example, "You believe you can stay up all of the night studying and do well on the exam the next day. How are you going to handle the fatigue and lack of concentration that come from not having enough rest?" is better than "You're crazy! There's no way you can stay up all night and think straight the next day. You'll be a basket case!"

   In general, avoid the third degree and use a little gentle hu-mor where appropriate. If our children perceive us as the enemy, they are very likely to resist our efforts to help.

   It is important to note that steps 4 through 8 are excellent for students to learn and use permanently as means of solving academic problems. Ultimately, the goal is for them to be able to use this procedure independently, without having to rely on adults except as valued partners or resources in their efforts.

Role of the Teacher

   In addition to being part of the problem-solving process it-self, when necessary, teachers can restructure their instructions so that they encourage successful learning for those who are willing to expend the effort. Again, we want to caution the parents reading this book that what we are about to suggest is often more an issue of the teacher having the necessary time rather than the necessary skill.

   Some students may be discouraged when they realize how much extra time and effort will be needed to improve. However, teachers can positively influence their attitudes when they can guarantee the following three conditions, which are based on mastery learning:[5]

1. Varied, quality instruction that will help students to learn if they try to learn. In addition to the main instructional techniques—lectures, discussion, reading assignments—have some alternatives available to meet the needs of individual students. Some alternative techniques might include:

- *Small cooperative group study procedures* on an as-needed basis that require two or three students to meet regularly to go over points of difficulty in learning a subject.
- *Other suggested textbooks* that may offer a clearer or more extensive discussion of the material the students are having difficulty grasping in the adopted textbook.
- *Programmed instruction and computer-assisted instruction* that provide the drill and specific tasks that regular instruction cannot. Some students need small steps and frequent feedback to overcome particular learning difficulties.
- *Audiovisual methods* that can provide illustrations and vivid explanations often not found in regular learning materials.
- *Tutorial help* is often a last resort, but if teachers can make this available or guide students to such outside resources, this is certainly very helpful to many students.

2. Concrete evidence that student effort makes a difference. See condition 3 for examples.

3. Continual feedback regarding the progress of learning. Conditions 2 and 3 are frequently integrated as a process.

- *Focusing on personal improvement* helps students remember that almost everyone can succeed at "getting better." This enables students to have a chance for more frequent success when their own learning progress becomes the basis for measuring gains in learning.
- *Graphing or charting progress* makes it more concrete and shows a record of increasing improvement.

- *Shortening the interval before feedback is given* helps students to maintain motivation and concentration. For example, doing three problems with the knowledge that feedback will be given soon may be much more attractive than doing ten problems before feedback is initiated.

- *Segmenting learning into smaller units* allows progress to be more easily understood by the learner. Counting how many laps you have run gives a quicker sense of progress than counting by the mile. The same is true for counting how many pages you have read versus how many chapters have been read.

- *Frequent use of formative evaluation* would include diagnostic exams and tests that are not graded. They assess student progress, indicate points of learning difficulty, and reveal learning mastery as well. Such materials allow students opportunities for positive feedback and corrective strategies with no penalty. This lets students be aware of what they know and what they can do to help themselves.

Appropriately used, retesting, contracts, extra assignments, and mastery learning conditions can give the students who want to improve a greater sense of self-determination and competence. One of the documented results of these conditions is that they tend to increase students' interest in the subject.[6] Thus people can become interested in things they *eventually decide* to do well.

Encouragement

Parents and teachers can each offer encouragement in their own domains, as well as together. In all instances the rules are the same. Parents have the advantage of greater intimacy and emotional bonding. For both the teacher and the parent, the primary foundations for encouragement are our caring and our acceptance of the young person. We can encourage a student in these ways:

1. *Give recognition for real effort.* We have already said a great deal about this aspect of encouragement. It is fundamental and it is first on the list.

2. *Demonstrate a confident and realistic expectancy that the young person will learn* (discussed in Chapter Three).
3. *Emphasize learning from mistakes* (discussed in Chapter Three).

Much of the "fountainhead" for motivation to learn developing into a personal trait is an encouraging environment, and much of the support system for young people who want to overcome lack of success in learning is a stream from those same waters.

4. *Be available, especially at the beginning of difficult tasks.* It is amazing what can be lifted and moved with just a little help. Sometimes a student might have a momentary confusion or not know what to do next. Our proximity and minimal assistance can be just enough for the young person to find the right direction, continue involvement, and gain the initial confidence to proceed with learning.
5. *Minimize mistakes while the young person is struggling.* Sometimes learning is like a battle. The critical line between advancement and withdrawal, or between hope and despair, is tenuous at best. Emphasis on a young person's mistakes at such a critical moment is accentuated by his or her vulnerability and is a sure way to promote self-defeat.

One of the striking implications of theories and research about encouragement is how important adult availability is. Most of the more specific practices of encouragement cannot be carried out unless a caring adult is present.

At the heart of dealing with lack of success in learning is an interlocking of the efforts of the student, the teacher, and the parents. It starts where it probably started centuries ago, with a strong thread of gumption and good problem-solving strategy. Teaching methods that engender determination and mastery are a more recent element in this network. And yet the cord that holds all this together—encouragement—can be traced to ancient times. In their writings, Cicero and Seneca refer to "kindness to the good" as a noble trait. Seneca wrote, "All mankind is beholden to him who is kind to the good." Is that not what encouragement is? A seeking and supporting of the better and healthier qualities in someone. To encourage children is beyond common sense or the mere expediency of another helpful educational method that might work. It is wisdom.

Chapter 7

——8——

Reducing Anxiety
Over Tests and Grades

Anxiety and conscience are a powerful pair of dynamos. Be-
tween them, they have ensured that I shall work hard, but they
cannot ensure that one shall work at anything worthwhile.

—Arnold J. Toynbee

"YOU'RE HAVING YOUR FINAL EXAM TOMORROW." For many students, that message strikes with the impact of a falling blacksmith's anvil. The emotions rise. Panic can be sensed. Tears are shed. Doors are slammed and locked. Students take on the sensitivity of nitrogly-cerin. Any disturbance, and they might explode.

This is painful and sad for everyone. Students are distressed. They feel apprehensive, distracted, and irritable. Parents feel help-less and worried. Not only do they fear for the health of their chil-dren but they also realize how impaired their performance will be on the exam if their anxiety does not subside. They offer words of re-assurance, knowing that what afflicts their children is much like a fever. It will pass only when the exam is over. Teachers feel frus-trated and guilty. They are the wardens of the exams. They under-stand the limitations of the exams and know that some of their stu-dents will perform significantly below their capabilities because their anxiety interferes with their concentration and memory.

The constant looming threat of judgment by exam is one of the biggest reasons motivation to learn is so difficult to establish as an enduring desire among American students. The older students get, the more they are ranked and sorted by exams. Say what we will about how wonderful learning is, the students know that what counts, what gains for them their promotions and career opportunities, are their exam scores. That reality is a fist in the stomach of intrinsic motivation because the goal of learning is obviously highly external and very controlling.[1]

Keeping your motivation to learn and dealing with the onslaught of exams in American schools is like learning to live with the troll at the bridge. You cannot cross it unless you pay him his due, but learning has so many riches that you will find the payment if you continue to learn. The problem is that the troll really worries you.

Approximately 10 million elementary and secondary students have difficulty in evaluative situations because of anxiety.[2] This condition appears pervasive in college as well.[3] It has been identified as a widespread educational problem that requires attention. *Test anxiety* is defined as an unpleasant feeling or emotional state that has physiological and behavioral side effects and that is experienced in formal testing or other evaluative situations.[4] Worry and autonomic responses such as sweating, upset stomach, and heartpounding are its trademarks. Test anxiety appears to be a learned condition that can begin as early as the third grade and be firmly in place by the fifth grade.[5] It is a problem for children from all major sociocultural groups in our society.

Ray Hembree's recent comprehensive review of the research on test anxiety is disturbing in both its findings and its implications.[6] Highly test-anxious students hold themselves in lower esteem than do those students who have low test anxiety. They tend to feel unprotected and controlled by outside forces and are prone to other forms of anxiety. They have difficulty with concentrating, staying on task, and remembering concepts. They become overly preoccupied with doing poorly when being evaluated by tests of any sort, recitation, and new or difficult learning tasks. Thus there is a serious problem in terms of their motivation, and they do not show optimal performance during tests because of the interference of their anxiety. Such anxious students do not perform up to their capabilities. Measures such as standardized achievement tests and grades on report cards underestimate their knowledge, skills, and learning.

General Solutions to Prevent Evaluation Anxiety

We begin by discussing what parents and schools can do in a global manner to help students to be motivated and self-confident when they are being evaluated. Some of what we suggest is critical of current trends in educational policy and structure because we believe many grading and testing practices have reached a point of diminishing returns.[7] In addition to recitation, classroom quizzes and exams, and standardized achievement tests, most school districts have added minimal competency testing to determine promotion. Also, nationwide there is an increased use of test scores to evaluate educational programs and to track students according to levels of ability and achievement.

These are not diagnostic quizzes. These are often exams with serious consequences for students. As a result of their performance on these tests, some of them do not graduate, do not get promoted, and do not get into the gifted and talented program. (Does that make them mediocre and dull?) On standardized tests, it is automatic that 50 percent of them will not be able to claim title to that most profoundly reassuring level of humanity called "above average." We think a necessary first step for reducing the negative effects of evalution anxiety may be for parents and teachers to ask, "What is the testing policy of our school and how is it affecting the motivation of our students?"

Report card grades are another important way of documenting progress in learning. Though most of the research on evaluation anxiety has focused on test performance, Kennedy Hill and Seymour Sarason found that anxiety was significantly related to report card grades as well.[8] Traditional letter grades can have a negative impact on many students' motivation to learn. They are often misleading. Single A, B, C, D, and F grades for each subject provide little diagnostic information and may reflect teachers' evaluation of students across several dimensions, including learning, effort, and conduct. If a normative grading system is used, students are unfairly denied access to success and may be forced into a form of competition with their peers that is neither enjoyable nor useful.

A well-designed report card is informative about students' progress in learning and encourages their motivation to learn.[9] If letter grades are used, there should be separate comments for *achievement* (quality of progress in learning), for *effort* (quality of diligence and persistence), for *strengths* (positive factors such as creativity, communication skills, and areas of special expertise), for *areas to improve* (knowledge and skills in need of strengthening and refinement), and for *social development* (characteristics such as cooperation, maturity, and class participation). Such remarks emphasize that the purpose of school is learning rather than receiving a particular grade.

In general, competition and social comparison should be minimized in grading practices.[10] If introduced at all, letter grades can easily be delayed until the last two years of elementary school. Written progress reports can replace grades and are often used in early elementary school. (See Resource E.) With younger children, parents and teachers seem to intuitively realize how just giving a single letter as a grade increases negative competition and self-demeaning thinking among students. However, this is probably no less true for older children as well.

At any grade level, the criteria for grades should be explained clearly so students can judge and plan their work to meet standards that are valued by them. Such clarity is equally important for students' improvement when the grades are not satisfactory to them. If ways to improve and raise grades are evident to students, they will be much more likely to believe that effort and determination will make a useful difference.

As mentioned earlier, in Chapters Four and Six, parents can do a great deal to create conditions that lessen the chances that their children will become severely anxious about grades or overly distressed as a result of the grades they receive. By emphasizing realistic expectations for their children in terms of what they can achieve within the bounds of their talent and effort, parents put the odds for satisfactory grades in favor of their children and create self-fulfilling prophecies that are more likely to lead to higher aspirations. By *not* comparing their children's grades to those of other students, they concretely model that the learning of their own children concerns them most. This reduces unfair pressure on children and allows them to see their parents' reactions as respecting them as individuals and doing what is best for their personal development. By valuing their children's effort to learn beyond the grade received for achievement, they respect their children's dignity. In this manner their children can always save face and not fall victim to giving up because they fear perseverance will only make whatever ability they might lack more evident. Recent notable studies have shown that judging children primarily on their ability in school will lead those children who are trying hard but still not doing well to stop trying.[11] And finally, by treating grades as information, parents leave the door wide open for effective problem solving when their children are dissatisfied with the standards their school performance indicates. This develops hope and gumption in their children.

Specific Methods to Reduce Evaluation Anxiety

One of the major influences on evaluation anxiety is the testing procedure the teacher uses.[12] The way tests are planned, constructed, timed, and introduced has an impact on the anxiety level of the students who take them. Time limits and time pressure create stress, especially among anxious children who prefer to perform slowly and cautiously. Emphasizing that a test measures ability can lead anxious students to be overly concerned about the adequacy of their performance on the test. Some students lose confidence and concentration when they run into a series of test items that appear extremely difficult to them. They may infer that they are certain to do poorly on such an exam and disregard the merit of their work on the remainder of the exam.

Teachers can use the following guidelines to prevent and lessen the emergence of evaluation anxiety among students. Although testing is stressed, these suggestions are applicable to any evaluation situation ranging from recitation to a paper-and-pencil exam.

1. Use competition very carefully.[13] All three of the following items tend to increase evaluation anxiety: (1) public exposure of ability, (2) lack of a reasonable chance for success, and (3) significance of the meaning or goal of winning. Simply stated, no one likes to lose, especially when he looks bad and knew he would before he even started.

2. Make sure instructions are clear. Write exam instructions on the board or on the test itself instead of giving them orally. When giving any form of evaluation, check with students to be sure they understand. Ask a few students how they would do the first item and correct any misperceptions. For any new format or new type of task, give the students clear examples as models to show how it is done. Such clarity helps students to concentrate on what they know rather than to use their energy to figure out how they should proceed.

3. Avoid unnecessary time pressure and time limits.[14] Basically, this means all students need to be able to complete all important classroom tests within the time limits given. There may be two exceptions. One is standardized tests. We realize teachers may have little choice where these are concerned; however, time pressure is one of the severe limitations of standardized exams. The other is diagnostic tests, in which time spent has some informational value. Studies indicate that when time limits are relaxed, anxious students perform better than when time limits are rigid and about as well as less anxious students do.[15]

4. Introduce exams with encouragement rather than threat. This means avoid emphasis on difficulty, comparison with others, relationship to grades, and the use of the exam as a true measure of ability. Teachers can help students to feel more relaxed and confident when they introduce exams as opportunities for which students have been well prepared and upon which they can competently perform. Emphasis should be on the test as a means for students and teachers to realize the progress of their learning. In this regard, teachers can convey an attitude that students perceive as supportive and optimistic. As teachers, we are saying to them, "You will do well. And we are rooting for you."

5. Make preparation for the evaluation evident. Because the main goal of evaluation is to offer students an opportunity to give the best evidence of their learning, how to prepare to offer this evidence should be clear to them. Teachers can indicate what to study, how to prepare, and how to self-evaluate one's learning. For example, for a forthcoming history exam, the students know the chapters on which the exam will be based and the main points that have been emphasized. In addition, the teacher has given them a study guide with sample questions and answers that they can use for practice and to check their understanding. Exams that are a mystery to students undermine their effort, increase their anxiety, and too often reflect a lack of purpose in what is being taught.

Students can learn test-taking skills and motivational dispositions that can help them cope with the demands and pressures of testing. The suggestions in the following outline are applicable from the second grade through college. These skills and attitudes can be learned from parents or teachers. Each will have to be adjusted to the particular subject and testing situation. These generalizations are largely based on a successful teaching program reported by Kennedy Hill and Allan Wigfield in the *Elementary School Journal*.[16]

Test-Taking Skills and Motivational Dispositions

I. General Test Skills and Knowledge
    A. Be comfortable. This applies to how you dress, where you sit, and how you write, including pencils and pens that are convenient to your grip.
    B. Sit where you can easily hear and see what is important. If you cannot understand something because it is not clear to you, bring this to the teacher's attention as soon as possible.
    C. Pay careful attention to the teacher.
    D. The teacher can help you understand how to work on a test, but cannot tell you answers for the test.
    E. The purpose of most tests is to find out what you know and what you have learned. This information can help your teacher to teach better and you to learn better.
II. Positive Motivation: Doing Your Best
    A. Do your best. This benefits you and your teacher because it gives the soundest evidence of what you actually have learned and how you can be helped to learn more. Your test performance also represents your work and effort in which you take personal pride.
    B. If you finish your test before time is up, go back and

check your answers. This bonus allows you to refine and edit your work.

C.   When you feel tension beginning to develop, stop a moment, take a deep breath, and relax. Baseball pitchers often do this just before they wind up and deliver the ball. In a similar manner you are activating your mind and delivering the information you know.

III.   Positive Motivation: Self-Reassurance

A.   Some tests have some very difficult problems. Do not worry if you cannot do some problems. You are doing your best and can do no more.

B.   Some tests have problems that you will not understand. Do not worry. You may not have had a chance or enough time to learn this material. Just skip a problem if you do not understand it at all.

C.   If you work hard but do not finish a test, do not worry about it! The most important thing is that you concentrate and do as well as you can. All students can do their best if they keep at it. You will do a good job if you try!

IV.   Test Strategy and Problem-Solving Skills

A.   For most exams other than essay tests, there is only *one* best answer.

B.   If you do not know the right answer but have some idea, choose or write the answer that you *think* is best. This gives you a chance for some credit for what you know.

C.   Do what you know first. If you cannot answer a question or a problem or it is taking a lot of time, move on to the next one. You can come back later if you have time.

D.   Do not rush. If you work *too fast,* you can make careless errors. You have to work carefully.

E.   Do not work too slowly. Do your answers and problems at a moderate rate.

F.   On complex tests or those with many items, keep track of where you are working on the page by keeping one hand on this spot.

G.   Before you begin writing on essay tests, think through each answer, organize your thoughts, and find clear examples for your ideas.

Identifying and Helping Test-Anxious Students

Most students are capable of becoming anxious about a particular test or evaluation situation. However, some students are frequently anxious about testing and do poorly under evaluative pressure. On an individual basis, the IQs, aptitudes, and progress of such test-anxious students are consistently misinterpreted and undervalued. We suggest that parents and schools assess students systematically to identify students with test-taking problems. There are several measures of anxiety that are easy to administer.

One of the most cost-efficient questionnaires is the seven-item Test Comfort Index.[17] This scale, which can be administered to children at all grades, takes only five minutes to give. It is reliable and valid. Most of the questions in the seven-item instrument ask students how they feel during tests, for example, "Do you feel relaxed before you take a test?" The developers of this scale recommend its use with an attribution measure to find additional information regarding the students' beliefs about their test performance. For example, one item asks, "When you have done well on a test in school, is it usually because you tried very hard?" These two instruments provide an effective and inexpensive way to identify students with test-taking problems. They are available through Dr. Kennedy T. Hill, professor of educational psychology at the University of Illinois at Urbana-Champaign.[18] Hill and his colleagues have developed a five-hour, ten-session classroom teaching program to prepare students in general for testing, as well as an individualized tutoring program for students identified by teachers as being anxious and doing poorly on tests, especially in mathematics.

Test anxiety can be effectively reduced by a variety of treatments on either a group or individual basis.[19] These methods reduce both worry and physical symptoms such as perspiration and stomachache. They include systematic desensitization (the most common treatment reported in studies), relaxation training, hypnosis, cognitive modification, and stress inoculation. These methods are available through school counselors, therapists, and mental health clinics.

Improved test performance and higher grade-point average consistently accompany test-anxiety reduction.[20] Also, when children receive the treatments just described, their effects do not appear to decline with the passage of time. The children remain less anxious in evaluative situations and this condition is stable.

Students do not need to stagger through school with test anxiety. They can be helped in a number of ways that are inexpensive and efficient. They can experience success and enhance their motivation to learn. They can have a fairer chance to show what they know. At the very least, where tests are used for promotion or placement, test instructions and time limits must accommodate test-anxious students. Such an adjustment might include instructions that clarify the pattern of difficulty among test items, information about penalties for guessing, the need for pacing, and less severe time restrictions for completion of the test. If accommodations of this nature are not made for test-anxious students, the entire testing process is biased against them. Parents and teachers can work together to remedy this inequity.

Chapter 8

Overcoming Boredom and Indifference

Against boredom even the gods themselves struggle in vain.

—Friedrich Nietzsche

"BORING! IT'S BORING. That class is so dull it makes watching ice melt seem exciting." Children today have little difficulty telling us when they feel bored. Often they state it indignantly and with blameful gusto as though the adult world has conspired to make their lives petty and routine. Some people are actually intimidated by this. Yet, for centuries, boredom has been a nemesis of the quality of life almost everywhere. To escape its oppressive grasp is more rare than common; work and learning are two areas that typically seem especially vulnerable to the spontaneous emergence of this vague but powerful emotion. When we look at the causes of boredom, we begin to see why these two fields of endeavor are fertile ground for its occurrence.

Monotony is frequently a cause of boredom.[1] Doing the same thing over and over again without any appreciable change becomes dull, no matter how exciting it might seem in the first place. Learning, with its demands for practice and routine, can become quickly tedious to many students. Constraint contributes to boredom as well. When people feel confined, the tasks they are doing become more oppressive to them. Because so much of schooling occurs in large groups, control of students is often of paramount concern and restrictions to movement abound in most schools. Leaving your desk without permission is taboo in most classrooms. Meaninglessness increases boredom, too. When students do not perceive a valued purpose to their assignments, they will see the work as wearisome at best.

Lack of challenge is another quality that eventually can make work or learning a humdrum affair.[2] People feel stagnant when what they do demands too little of their ability and effort. However, it is in the area of challenging students that teachers walk a very tight line. Think of the last time you were truly challenged. Our hunch is that this incident had some degree of risk to it because the essence of challenge is the chance to fail. And the greater the challenge, the greater the chance for failure. In some ways, teachers are between the devil and the deep blue sea on the issue of challenge. If what they offer students is too challenging, the students may fail and the subsequent lack of success will diminish their motivation. If what they offer students is not challenging enough, their course work will appear dull and uninspiring. To find the right balance for thirty individuals is quite a challenge for most teachers!

By virtue of their size, requirement for routine, order, and practice, and typical population, schools are a natural haven for boredom. When we examine the reasons people will endure boredom, we begin to see that certain school practices that conflict with motivation to learn remain because of their power to control bored students. In most cases people in this culture endure boredom because of fear, pressure, extrinsic goals, and lack of alternatives.[3] In the workplace money and survival make boredom tolerable. In schools fear of failure and grades make boredom tolerable.

This is a bleak picture of schools. Yet if we are to increase students' motivation, we need to recognize how the emphasis on grades for extrinsic control diminishes students' spontaneous love of learning. Yet the emphasis on grades continues intact because grades are frequently seen as effective motivators in schools, where boredom can be a result of systematic mass education. Very few options exist for controlling students or giving them incentives under such circumstances. To diminish the need for grades and tests to act as extrinsic coercion on students means looking at who is responsible for boredom and what helps children to develop interests and to find learning stimulating.

The fact that young people can be profoundly bored by the most elaborate productions of classical drama, music, and dance is an important lesson for us as parents and teachers. More than a few intelligent older adolescents prefer the Smurfs to Shakespeare, Madonna to Beethoven, and the Solid Gold Dancers to Baryshnikov. What people find interesting and stimulating is to a major extent learned and subjective. What people find appealing is based on experience and exposure, as well as their present development, needs, memories, and current events in society. Parents have the greatest influence on what children are exposed to and what experiences they have. Thus one could convincingly argue that many students are not interested in school subjects because their parents have not taught them or prepared them to be interested in academic subjects. It is also logical then to take the position that such students might find a subject such as history, no matter how well taught, boring, just as they might find the finest Chekhov play boring because their parents have ill prepared them for anything demanding depth of understanding and concentration.

With this evidence and logic, we can begin to see that schools are not entirely responsible for the possible boredom of their students. Parents play a crucial role in influencing what students will find stimulating. As we have so often previously emphasized, parents and teachers are inextricably joined in their responsibility for what young people are motivated to learn, from the attitude they bring to school to the interest they find in a particular subject. As before, we will share what both teachers and parents can do mutually to help children to lessen their boredom and to find the genuine stimulation that learning infinitely offers.

Some Fair Questions for the Bored Student

We are not going to pretend. There are boring teachers, and there are textbooks whose contents would make reading a candy wrapper fascinating by comparison. However, we take the position that every teacher should get a fair chance. In addition, seldom will most students be able to change their teachers and even more rarely will they be able to change their textbooks. Making an apparently boring learning situation more stimulating is making the best of it for everyone concerned. Students will learn more and teachers will give more. In some ways this is also a form of creative problem solving, a fine asset in any walk of life.

Unless the student is in class to be entertained, stimulation is a two-way street. It is reciprocal, much like a conversation. To be stimulated people have to participate in earnest. Thus we believe a fair question for anyone who complains of boredom is "How do you contribute to your own boredom?" And a fair admonition is "Come on, now. You can help yourself with this." We would hope that the young person would ask, "How?" Whether or not that happens, we think the following questions are helpful to a parent and child discussing the problem of boredom and, as we have advocated earlier, approaching it as a couple of detectives gamely solving a problem.

Are you up to date on your studying and homework? Students cannot be stimulated by what they do not understand or are not prepared to comprehend. Being behind in homework and studying often creates a gap between what the student knows and what the teacher has to offer. The material is not very interesting because the student lacks the necessary knowledge to appreciate it.

Do you pay attention? Most young people would answer yes to this question. Or maybe, "Yes, but it's like watching paint dry." A no is blatantly self-incriminating. Yet it is important to ask this question because if the parents consult the teacher at a later date, the student would feel embarrassed and resistant if lack of paying attention were the contributor to boredom. "Do you sometimes *not* pay attention?" might be a good follow-up or starter question. This is less intimidating and allows for some exploration into what the student does when he or she is not paying attention, which may have real value for solving the boredom problem.

Are you having success in the class? Sometimes boredom is a smoke screen for lack of confidence or feelings of incompetence. It is easier and less derogatory to oneself to say, "It's boring," than to say, "I'm not doing well or as well as I'd like to do." If there appears to be less success in learning than the young person desires, then solving this issue may lead to resolving boredom.

Do you participate when you have a chance to participate? One of the main things that can keep a person stimulated while learning when the learning does not appear initially interesting is to participate when the chance occurs. Giving opinions or answers, entering the discussion, and going to the chalkboard stimulate the student because he or she is responding, has to be socially aware to continue, and feels more accountable and less passive. All of these activities increase interest and raise the alertness of the student. One of the best ways for teachers to maintain students' attention is to ask questions at random of the class and direct some to individuals so that everyone has a chance to participate.[4] Helping your child to find ways to participate constructively more frequently may genuinely increase the child's interest in the class.

Do you ask questions? A good question is thoughtful, and a good thought is stimulating. Asking questions demands thinking. When a person creates questions about what he or she is learning, the person becomes more involved because that individual is actively doing something with the information received, rather than the proverbial "letting it go in one ear and out of the other."[5] Encouraging your child to ask one or two thoughtful questions, especially ones that apply the knowledge being learned during class, will increase the child's involvement and interest. Just writing questions about what the teacher is teaching perks up a student. It could be a lot of fun for a parent and a child to spend part of the evening going over and discussing the questions the child has thought of as a result of a day in school.

Do you take notes and write personal examples when the teacher lectures? Teachers who lecture should be very good lecturers and even then use other methods to involve their students. Lecturing is like television. It tends to keep students in a passive state. Because most students watch so much television, the context of their perception of a lecturing teacher is all those television programs and movies. Against a background filled with "Sesame Street," Bill Cosby, and MTV, the average lecturing teacher is dull. Taking notes while the teacher lectures increases the student's involvement because the student must pay closer attention and transform the information into his or her own words.[6] By including personal examples of what the teacher is lecturing about, the student applies the knowledge being learned, which deepens the level of thinking and adds an emotional touch. Emotions tend to heighten interest.

The next two questions are exclusively for homework.

If you are allowed to write in your book, do you underline important passages while reading your textbook? Doing so increases concentration and involvement because the student is not only reading to comprehend but also evaluating the importance of the material at the same time. Studies indicate that underlining can be effectively employed by students at the seventh grade level and higher.[7]

Do you write personal examples and applications of what you are studying? Just as in the lecturing example, applying the knowledge being learned and elaborating it by adding your own examples deepens the level of thinking and heightens interest.[8] An example might be a student who, while reading about the concept of a phobia for the first time, reflects on personal irrational fears and writes "spiders" in the margin of his or her notes. For students, the personal creation of a good example of what is being read in a textbook is a "moment of truth" for personal understanding. Making an example is a way of making a connection that clarifies, applies, and accentuates the information or concept studied. Such concrete examples reinforce the student's awareness of personal competence and stimulate thinking.

The questions offered thus far point to a basic generalization in learning: The more successful and mentally, emotionally, and physically involved the student is, the more unlikely it is that boredom will occur.[9] Parents and their children can play an active part in reducing boredom. Now we take a closer look at the role of the teacher.

Some Methods of Teaching That Make Learning More Stimulating

If the student is willing to put forth the necessary effort, the teacher has a responsibility to help that child feel successful. All of the following methods are based on this premise. We also believe that rarely should students be bored in school for extended periods of time if they can answer affirmatively the questions we have asked in the previous sections of this chapter. The more that parents and their children accept their responsibility for their roles in learning and the more they understand what effective teaching is, the more

they will get what they deserve—a competent and satisfying education for the young people of this society. To paraphrase Pat Cross of
the University of California, Berkeley, we need responsible gourmet
learners, people who are selective about the kind of education they
receive and who are willing to do their part and act cooperatively to
receive it.[10]

Before we discuss some of the methods that make learning
more stimulating, we want to emphasize that different subjects need
to be taught differently because the structure of the subject matter is
so dissimilar. Teaching chemistry is not at all like teaching spelling. Therefore the methods we will offer are generic—teachers can
use them with just about any grade level and any subject. Yet some
teachers may not use them because the methods they currently use
are effective and *specific* to their subject area, such as the use of
experiments in chemistry. Nonetheless, we believe both parents and
teachers should know these methods because they can then mutually support their practice in school and possess a common ground
of understanding to solve problems of motivation with students.

Successful learning and enthusiastic teaching are essential
ingredients for all of the methods that follow:

Provide variety in learning.[11] Well-timed changes in methods of instruction help students to pay attention and renew interest.
For example, going from a lecture to a discussion to a film and then
to an exercise requires students to think and act differently on each
occasion. The main thing is to avoid a tedious diet of the same kind
of lessons followed by the same kind of assignments, which turns
into the "daily grind."

Relate learning to student interests.[12] Every time teachers can
relate learning to what students find personally meaningful, the
more likely they will be to gain and hold their attention. The most
attractive and informative examples are those that vividly touch
upon what students already find interesting. For example, an English teacher asks her students to bring in the lyrics of their favorite
songs and uses them as a springboard to teaching twentieth-century
poetry.

Because student interests change so rapidly and because
youth is more and more a culture unto itself, we have included a
Student Interest Survey at the back of this book (see Resource F).

Teachers can use it to update their awareness of students' current fascinations.

Use unpredictability within safe bounds for learning.[13] When students feel basically safe but are not exactly sure about what might happen next, they can have a feeling of enjoyable excitement as well as anticipation. Teachers can plan the unexpected, make a "mistake" on purpose, act a bit out of character, tell a self-depre-cating story, and crack a joke now and then. With the right timing, even something as subtle as lecturing from a seat among the students can have a wonderful effect.

Use novel and unusual teaching methods and content with students.[14] Anything that gets students to ask, "How come?" will get them involved in learning. The goal is to have students feel a little perplexed and wondering. This will cause them to think harder and reflect more deeply. Ask questions like "Why is it that the world can produce enough food to feed everyone, yet starvation runs rampant even in countries with the highest standards of living?" or "If you look at a mirror your image reverses from left to right; why not from top to bottom?" Introducing contradictions, using experiments, and playing the devil's advocate are instructional processes that bring unusual and different information to students in an exciting way.

Give students questions and tasks that get them thinking beyond rote memory.[15] Questions and assignments that request students to apply what they have learned to solve realistic problems are excellent. For example, "According to the definition of *creativity* that we have studied, what do we do in class that could be classified as creative?" or "Which among the research designs we have studied would be the best one to study the effects of the serious air pollution we have in our country?" Getting students to use their minds to analyze something is stimulating for them: "Let's see if we can figure out why people often respond so differently to similar frustrations." Helping young people to act and think creatively is a wonderful way to involve them. *Predict, draw, construct, produce, origi-nate, propose, plan, design, combine, develop,* and *create* are some of the key verbs that are certain to be part of the dialogue between teachers who inspire creativity and their students. Also important is getting students to evaluate something. When students have to judge or appraise an idea, theory, or argument, they have to dig deeper mentally and use their knowledge as criteria for their opinions. That is partly what makes debates exciting and interesting for spectators as well as participants.

Have students actively participate in learning.[16] The key word is *actively*. The majority of students of any age level favor learning situations that allow them to participate actively rather than just to listen or to read. Activities that involve students and help to keep them alert include games, role playing, exercises, discussions, group projects, simulations, experiments, puzzles, field studies, and problems. Many of these activities are social by nature and that adds to the students' emotional involvement as well.

Provide consistent feedback.[17] *Feedback* is information that students receive about the quality of their performance on a given task. Knowledge of results, comments about skill performance, notes on a written assignment, and an approving nod are forms of feedback that teachers often use with students. Feedback is likely to enhance students' motivation because it allows them to evaluate their progress, to understand the level of their competence, to maintain effort toward realistic goals, to correct their errors, and to receive encouragement from their teachers.

Qualitatively, feedback is more likely to be motivating when it is:

> *Informational:* relates to the student's increasing mastery and indicates that the quantity and quality of learning are mainly determined by the student. For example, "You've cut your error rate in half, and that shows you've made real improvement."
>
> *Specific:* important descriptions and details are given, ranging from number of correct items to insightful commentary.
>
> *Corrective:* in general, the student is directed toward appropriate means of improvement.
>
> *Prompt:* is given as quickly as the occasion permits. Sometimes students are too emotionally involved or confused to be given immediate feedback. It might be better to wait

until they are more calm and clear about the task before
giving them feedback.

Positive: emphasizes improvement, progress, and correctness
rather than deficiencies and mistakes.

Timely: not necessarily frequent, but given when improvement is most possible, as when a student is beginning to
learn a skill.

Examining the criteria for motivating feedback, you can see
why personal computers can be so powerfully motivating with their
facility to provide unintimidating and objective, immediate feedback to the students using them.

**Create learning experiences that have natural consequences
or finished products.**[18] Natural consequences are any changes or
products that students can perceive as a direct result of their learning and effort. Solving a problem leads to the natural consequence
of arriving at an answer. Writing leads to a written product such as
an essay or letter. Building a model is an obvious display of a
finished product. Natural consequences and finished products concretely show students that their work has meaning and results. An-
ticipating and contributing to the development of the product leads
to a greater sense of involvement for students, and having a quality
product to show for their efforts increases their sense of pride.

Use cooperative learning techniques.[19] Cooperative learning
occurs when students perceive that they have a goal that they can
obtain if, and only if, the other students with whom they are linked
can obtain their goal.[20] Thus one student's success helps other students succeed, as in the case of a research team writing a single
paper or a group of students making a single project. Research
evidence shows that cooperative learning, when measured against
competitive learning and individualistic learning, can develop
greater trust among students, more emotional involvement, and
more commitment to learning, and can lower fear of failure.[21]

Cooperative learning experiences result in stronger beliefs
that one is liked, supported, and accepted by other students, and
that other students care about how much one learns and want to
help one another to learn.[22] Students in classes using cooperative
learning generally report liking their teachers better than do tradi-

tionally taught students.[23] This probably reflects the reality that it is more pleasurable to learn with supportive peers one likes and respects than to stand alone in a class of competitors.

Structuring cooperative learning involves, at minimum, the following steps once the learning goal is clear and desirable:[24]

1. *Proper group size:* For learning tasks, cooperative groups have the best chance for successful interaction when they have two to six members. Exceptions to this guideline are larger groups in which the purposes of interaction might be discussion, brainstorming, or some team game.

2. *Assignment of students to group:* In general, using random selection, such as having students count off and placing the "ones" together and the "twos" together, will result in a good variety of students in each group. Using this procedure to form different groups for different purposes should build good feelings of collaboration across the entire learning group. Sometimes, because of such reasons as interest in a specific topic or proximity outside of class, cooperative groups may be formed on a self-selected basis.

3. *Structuring interdependence and cooperation:* It is important that students fully understand that the activity is a cooperative one and that they need each other's contributions and support. This may take some guidance and practice for students who are unfamiliar with cooperation. In such cases smaller groups of two or three students should be used. Giving students a limited number of materials that they must share, such as lab equipment, in order to successfully reach their learning goal often makes working together much more obviously a helpful thing to do. The same principle applies to sharing books and information as well. Role interdependence in group projects can also work to develop individuals' skills, as when one student acts as the researcher, another as the writer, and another as the editor of a report.

4. *Monitoring and assistance:* Individual accountability and equal opportunity for learning are essential. All students must do their share. Getting a contract or outline with indicated responsibilities for each student can help to structure this. Ob-

serving and helping cooperative groups at the *beginning* is especially important because that is usually the most unstable time for them.

5. *Assessment:* Unless there is good reason to do otherwise, normal guidelines for evaluation can be used.

There are many different forms and variations of cooperative learning. Two excellent resources are *Learning Together and Alone,*[25] by David Johnson and Roger Johnson, and *Cooperative Learning,*[26] by Robert Slavin.

Encourage student choice in the learning situation.[27] Choice is the essence of responsibility. When students make choices, especially publicly, it is evident that they are, to an important extent, determining their behavior. This helps them to feel intrinsically motivated, positive, and accountable for their learning.

Choice is also a matter of degree and may be partial rather than full. It could mean selecting the topic and the partner one works with or the type of evaluation or the time of completion. A single assignment does not need to include all of these choices. Whenever making a choice gives a student a sense of willingness to learn, whether it be an outright commitment or a matter as seemingly routine as which group to join to play a game, it will encourage motivation.

In general, the more autonomous students feel, the more their intrinsic motivation can influence them. Sometimes, because students' decision-making skills may be limited, teachers may have to offer them a menu of choices or require them to get their choices approved before going on with the learning task.

Offer learning that is challenging.[28] To challenge anyone is not an easy thing to do. The recipient must be willing. The task must involve risk. The consequences are not altogether certain. So when today's media say that schools are not challenging enough, we think they usually mean they are not rigorous enough. They demand too little of students; the work required of students is too mundane and simple. We think many teachers might respond, "But when I have challenged my students, they did not want to do the work or take the chance."

To successfully challenge students means to help them to

want to do something that is at least moderately difficult to accomplish. *Moderately difficult* is a key concept in this definition. It means the students must apply reasonable effort or more to be successful at the task. It also means some degree of skill or strategy is necessary as well. The hardest aspect of offering challenges to students is to help them to *want* to accept the challenge. This means the learning or its result must somehow be desirable for the students. In essence, the teacher has to figure out how to make the difficult desirable.

All of the methods in this chapter that preceded this one are ways to make *the process* of learning desirable. Ways to make *the goal* of learning desirable mean making the results of learning or their meanings and consequences rewarding or important. For example, certain projects may emphatically tell students that they are competent or knowledgeable or skilled, such as publishing a class newspaper (uses writing, analysis, and drafting skills, among others), or conducting a survey about an issue of local interest (uses math skills and knowledge of statistics, among others). Another example might be having students study or research a topic that helps them to learn more about something they value. Sometimes the results of learning can become personally advantageous, for example, by helping students increase their interpersonal skills or improve their health.

Challenges are excellent opportunities for students to build their confidence and pride. They are invigorating experiences because they involve some risk. Work during a challenge can be filled with sweat, doubt, and anxiety: "Will I make it?" "How will it turn out?" Teacher support is very important at this time. And one of the most realistic ways to be supportive is to provide effective teaching that makes students' skills adequate to meet challenges that from their perspective are relatively high.[29] For example, a fascinating computer program can only be fascinating to the students who have learned programming skills.

We have discussed the process and the goal of challenges, but we must not forget the *context* of them as well. Evidence suggests that because academic challenges take place in school and involve formal learning, many adolescents are less likely to find them appealing.[30] A Bruce Springsteen lyric epitomizes this perception:

We busted out of class
　　had to get away from those fools.
We learned more from a three-minute record
　　than we ever learned in school.[31]

The way parents socialize their children to view school and to respect formal learning has a great deal to do with whether students regard schoolwork as compelling. Students who value learning are more easily challenged by it because it is desirable for its own sake. Their goal is further competence and evidence of it is appreciated. This is where we come full circle: Parents have the most responsibility for creating a value for learning within their children. Thus the student who is most likely to be challenged by learning probably embodies parental motivational influence. Looking only to schools to challenge students is shortsighted at best and unfair as well. Again, we see how intertwined the roles of the parent and the teacher are, even when the issue is boredom in the classroom.

Chapter 9

Encouraging Effort and Perseverance

When we do the best we can, we never know what miracle is wrought in our life, or in the life of another.

—Helen Keller

HOW MUCH EFFORT IS ENOUGH? At what point have we done our best? The voices of mythology, history, and science have always offered their heroic examples. From the *Odyssey* to the Alamo, and from Galileo atop his tower to Marie Curie in her laboratory, we have seen the mighty accomplishments of relentless perseverance. But alongside those images of inspirational attainment can emerge those unsettling realities of modern time—stress and burnout.

How much a student should persevere in school is a matter of subjective value. There is no valid scientific formula for the distribution of one's sweat and toil. However, the wisdom of an ancient thinker and a nineteenth-century novelist offers guidance that our experience supports as beneficial to motivation to learn.

In the first century before Christ, the Roman scholar Publilius Syrus wrote, "No one knows what he can do until he tries." This admonition reaches the core of motivation to learn because learning is a nurturing of potential, and effort is the ingredient that brings talent into bloom. Gaining confidence as a learner is a spiral in which one's effort and ability result in achievement and that achievement serves as the mental foundation for the next extension of effort and ability in learning. We do, and we believe we can do more. By not trying their best in learning, students deny themselves and their society the endowment of their gifts.

To try one's best in learning is better portrayed with visual images than with the traditional quantifiable exhortation to "give a hundred percent." Sometimes it is the concentrated force of a karate expert smashing a pile of bricks and sometimes it is the reflective musing of an artist watching clouds in the sky. Doing one's best as a student is bringing one's capacity—a dynamic combination of ability, effort, and strategy in the broadest sense—to fit the learning situation so that one's fullest potential is reached without doing damage. In some instances that might mean studying for six hours and in other instances that might mean sketching out a few ideas in a few minutes.

By "damage" we mean destruction to the student, to the relationship between the student and the subject matter (incurring a hatred for math or social studies, for example), or to those associated with the student in learning (feeling shame or distrust toward peers, teachers). Another way of expressing this concern is, When is trying our "best" trying too hard? Let us better understand how to make this judgment by using an analogy from the realm of physical strength. If you were to lift the greatest amount of weight you had ever lifted, you might do it, but the consequences might well be severely tearing some muscle tissue. You might succeed in achieving your personal best, but if you were to sustain a severe injury, it would likely prevent further development of your strength. The same principle is true for learning as well. In the attainment of a certain goal, such as achieving a particular score or grade, or completing a certain project or paper, a student could sustain an injury—psychological, physical, or social. Something may be gained, perhaps something grand, such as an award, but in the long run, something more is lost, such as a positive attitude toward the subject and, perhaps, the will to try that hard again. The following signs indicate that effort for learning probably has reached the point of diminishing returns:

> *Physical illness:* Depletion of energy is such that the body's resistance to illness is threatened.
>
> *Mental distress:* The student feels overwhelmed, extremely anxious, and unable to concentrate. Taking a break does not alleviate the symptoms.

Inefficiency: Things cannot be done well or successfully within normal time limits; ten minutes go into doing a math problem that usually takes five minutes; four minutes are required to read a page that usually takes one minute.

Loss of quality: The results of the learning effort become inferior—writing is less creative or the solutions to problems are wrong or inadequate.

Fatigue: The student is so tired that concentration is impaired.

Inability to cooperate: Ability to learn successfully or work with one's peers or teachers is visibly eroding.

Further wisdom in the realm of effort and learning comes from the pen of Robert Louis Stevenson, who wrote, "To travel hopefully is a better thing than to arrive, and the true success is to labor." Effort must have its own dignity if the act of learning is to thrive. Learning is an industrious endeavor. By nature, it is a striving. It can be fun and it can be very enjoyable, but no matter what the subject, there will be times of exertion and struggle. Most learning takes place through reading, studying, writing, computing, and critical thinking. Motivation to learn is a desire to discover, create, and toil. To be motivated to labor in this manner means to find satisfaction in the strenuousness of learning as the true athlete finds satisfaction in the exertion of exercise. To a large extent, this satisfaction for both the learner and the athlete emerges from a respect each possesses for the effort it takes to meet such a demand.

However, to encourage effort in learning, the wise course is to avoid tying the value of effort only to successful learning; when success is not enough or not forthcoming, the dignity of effort is unnecessarily diminished. Students who come to believe that effort is only worthwhile when successful learning is achieved will not exert effort when success seems unlikely. Martin Covington and Richard Beery capture well the dynamics of students in the classroom as they navigate to appear successful:

In the minute-by-minute reality of classroom life, each student is constantly changing his achievement strategies depending on events. One moment we may find a student trying all out on an assignment—in effect, seizing at success with both hands—because the odds are favorable to him; yet in the next instant his paramount concern is to play it safe, perhaps by waiting for others to answer the teacher's question before committing himself. Such a nonstop performance is worthy of a virtuoso. It is played out largely at an unconscious level with virtually automatic moves and countermoves that depend on the student's intuitive estimates of success and the stakes involved. . . .Yet for all the complexity involved, this drama has but one central purpose—the protection of the individual's sense of worth and dignity [pp. 61-62].[1]

Another benefit in valuing effort itself in learning is that it gives dignity to everyone who sincerely tries to learn. Students are not put down because their accomplishment is less than what someone else has achieved. They have tried their best, and they have the respect of their parents and their teachers. If this is not so, there is little reason to try their best.

Beyond building and maintaining their dignity, students who value effort for its own sake, and realize that they know how to work hard to learn, gain confidence, which, figuratively speaking, puts their reservoir for energy at the top of the hill rather than at the bottom. Parents who have reared children to believe that the main reason to exercise effort in learning is to achieve an extrinsic goal, such as an A grade, have to convince their children of two things: (1) getting an A has value and (2) getting an A is possible. If their children do not believe that getting an A is worthwhile or do not have the confidence to get an A, their motivation to learn will probably decline. In this manner, these parents have unknowingly set a trap for themselves and their children. They will have to pressure their children constantly to work hard because they must use coercion to overcome the negative effects of setting a goal for their children that the children may neither desire nor expect to achieve. By emphasizing extrinsic goals for learning—anything not directly a part of the effort and learning itself—parents inadvertently place the reservoir of their children's energy for learning at the bottom of the hill and have to continuously find goals (or hope their children will) to use to pump up their children's motivation to learn. Pardon the pun, but this is an uphill struggle.

By valuing effort and learning for their own sakes and helping their children to realize they can work hard and receive dignity in any learning situation, parents can help to place the reservoir for their children's learning at the top of the hill. All they have to do is help their children to find the proper channel for learning so the children's energy can flow with a sense of progress and accomplishment. Using another figure of speech, we might see such children as in shape for learning. Like well-conditioned athletes, they need to learn specific skills in order to participate in various events, but their fundamental stamina for endurance is not in question. Therefore we advocate that students try their best, and we realize full well that this is much more likely to occur when parents and teachers have continuously respected and supported students' effort as a valuable resource in its own right.

Approaching Problems of Insufficient Effort

We believe that the approach to a problem of insufficient effort is as important as the process used to solve the problem. The approach sets the tone and the structure for the entire process and its consequences. Either the teacher or the parent may decide there is a problem because of lack of effort. The following guidelines suggest forms of action that parents and teachers can incorporate in their styles of helping young people:

1. *Document the evidence for your concern.* One of the worst things you can do is accuse someone who is trying of *not* trying. Think of the last time someone did that to you. At the very worst, it can bring forth rage and, at the very least, it is insulting. Such mistaken accusations or insinuations do not make children charming. Such indirect signs as lower test scores and poorer grades may be due to difficult material or lack of prerequisite skills. Evidence such as decreased studying time or incomplete homework is much more appropriate. Either the parent or the teacher should begin by seeking information to solve a problem, not to accuse a student. In gathering such data, other clues to the solution may be discovered.

2. *While gathering data, diagnose the learning situation for*

lack of success, evaluation anxiety, and boredom. Most students will be motivated to learn and put forth sufficient effort if they can be successful, avoid fear of failure, and find a sense of self-determination and challenge in learning. Lack of effort may be symptomatic of a problem in one of these three areas. A discussion with the student that draws on approaches from the previous three chapters, such as guidelines for dealing with lack of success or boredom, may lead to changes that do not directly prescribe increased effort yet nonetheless result in greater perseverance on the part of the student.

3. The atmosphere for the entire process among the parents, teacher, and student should be one of mutual concern, cooperation, and gumption. We have discussed gumption and cooperation at length in previous chapters. At this point, we want to reiterate our cautions against panic and the tendency to place blame. Efforts to solve the problem that don't bring immediate results should be viewed as experiments in a difficult process. These "mistakes" will tell what needs to be tried next. People are at the meeting to help each other. All are demonstrating *mutual concern,* by which we mean a genuine interest in the welfare of the student, as well as the parent and teacher. People are not at the meeting to place blame, and everyone should have a chance to improve his or her situation as a result of the meeting. People at the meeting need to be sensitive about how they speak to each other and everyone needs to have a chance to voice his or her views. The process is as important as the product. This is not a shape-up mission.

4. If the parents and the teacher are to become involved in solving the problem, they should meet before attempting to resolve the problem with the child. The model for this is what two parents would typically do if they were concerned about one of their children. They would compare their ideas and evidence about the problem. They would discuss what information they need from the child and consider possible solutions and interventions. They would create some plan to proceed. We add two qualifiers.

The first qualifier is that the plans and ideas agreed upon by the parents and teacher need to remain open and flexible to the participation and perspective of the student. This is consistent with the first guideline in Chapter Three regarding the role of the authoritative parent. The parents and the teacher want to be reasonably organized, clear about their concerns, and in mutual agreement about their outside limits. Yet they also want the student's participation and perspective so that the solution makes sense to that person, as well, and is something that the student can truly believe he or she has had some part in determining. This will enhance cooperation and motivation throughout the process.

The second qualifier is that if the student becomes belligerent, the parents and teacher need to remain united in their mutual support of one another. Human beings frequently become hostile when they feel threatened or frustrated, or when they simply do not like what they may have to do. Belligerence from the student can often lead to conflict among the adults. Parents may respond to a child's anger with protectiveness that stems from fear of being perceived as disloyal and insecurity about their role and their agreement with the teacher. The teacher, also, may feel confused or abandoned. If the student sees that the adults are antagonistic or in basic disagreement, this further fuels the student's opposition because there appears to be growing support for, or at least less resistance to, the student's belligerent stance. If this happens, the student is likely to see resistance and hostility as tools in a power struggle in which time is on the student's side. By standing firm together, parents and teacher exude a confidence and a unity that both symbolically and functionally increase the student's understanding that a foundation of conviction and caring supports these adults in their commitment to help the student. Implied in this commitment is a value: Adults have the responsibility of preventing children from seriously harming themselves.

Solving Problems of Insufficient Effort

Although parents and teachers could use the following guidelines independently, we will offer all of our examples based on the assumption that parents and teachers are working collaboratively to increase student effort. Our numbering sequence will continue as an extension of the order begun in the preceding section. For the sake of consistency, all examples will deal with studying or homework.

5. In a personal manner, give your evidence and concerns about the student's insufficient effort. All adults present should explain their awareness of the evidence and concerns about insufficient effort and its consequences. For example, "Pat, you've stopped turning in your assignments. Even though I've reminded you, nothing's changed. And your participation in class has decreased. This means that your grade is definitely going to be lower. I'm concerned because you're not getting as much out of the course as you can. The material is important and beneficial to your understanding of today's world. Also, the lower grade could reduce some of your options for next semester. I wanted you to know that I wouldn't feel right about standing on the sidelines and just watching this happen."

6. Ask for the student's perspective and judgment of the situation, indicating your need for the student's collaboration. We also want to know the student's evaluation of what is happening as well as how he or she sees the consequences of insufficient effort. For example, "Pat, now that you know what we understand and feel about the situation, how do you see it? We need to know how you understand what is going on. What do you think about this?" If Pat has not addressed the issues of the incomplete assignments, or lower participation in class, or less understanding of important information and possible consequences, the adults can ask for further clarification. For example, "Pat, you haven't said anything about participating less in class. Could you clarify that for me?"

The timing of the request for the student's collaboration should be based on the personal judgment of the parents and teacher. Sometimes it is not even necessary to state such an appeal because the empathy intrinsic in the request for the student's perspective implies that this will be a collaborative effort. If there is some mistrust on the student's part, it may be better to say it earlier. For example, "Pat, I want to emphasize how important it is for us to solve this problem together. We need to know your point of view, and we need to work with you to find ways that you believe will help you complete these assignments."

It is usually beneficial to clarify excuses the student may offer. Counter expressions such as "I can't," "I don't know," or "I'm too slow" by asking what information is needed or what materials are necessary or what skills are lacking in order to expend the necessary effort. "Pat, you say you don't know how to find the time to do these assignments. How do you spend your time after school until you go to sleep?" This helps the student to identify where the boundary is for the responsibility the student has for his or her own effort.

When it's possible to do so sincerely, it is helpful for adults to indicate empathy regarding the student's reasons for lack of effort. For example, "I can see, Pat, why you would want to wait until you could do some of these assignments at the library. It would give you a chance to use more references. That shows you care about the quality of your work." Most people believe they do the best they can do and can find reasons to justify having done something in a particular way. Showing empathy for this helps the adults to create a feeling of collaboration with the student. Our approach in this section is to treat students the way we would like to be treated if a group of adults who had responsibility for us genuinely believed we were not putting enough effort into our work and met with us about it.

Guideline number 6 should lead to clarification of the situation. Now, with a teamlike feeling and to the extent necessary, follow the steps for problem solving discussed in Chapter Six, beginning with number 3: *Emphasize the positive side of the situation.* For example, "You know, Pat, this may sound kind of strange, but for myself, I'm looking forward to working with you to solve this problem about the assignments. I think you'll learn something about how to better manage your efforts. That should help you in future classes as well. And I'll probably learn some things that I can use to help the other kids, too." As stated earlier, the time for gumption and creativity has arrived. Enjoy it.

Goal Setting

Sometimes resolving a problem of insufficient effort leads to the establishment of a new goal. A student may need a better way to manage her time or do more studying, more reading, or more practicing. Goal setting is an effective individualized approach to increasing a person's expectations for successful accomplishment. We introduce it here as a means for increasing efforts to learn, but it can be used for achieving almost any goal and is a fine skill for any person to possess.

Goal setting, a form of planning, is very metacognitive. *Metacognition* is our ability to know what we know and what we don't know.[2] Most planning is metacognitive as we try to figure out the steps to reach a goal. Goal setting brings the future as much as possible into the present so we can carefully calculate what is necessary to avoid obstacles and to carry out strategies that lead to success. Goal setting gives people a better sense of self-determination and more confidence that they will reach their goal.

Let us say that Pat's problem was not having enough time to do the given assignments. The solution to the problem was for Pat to add one more hour each school evening for working on these assignments because they were a regular part of the course's procedure. That means Pat must find one additional hour on each of the five weekdays to do this homework. Pat realizes that the assignments are necessary, but feels overloaded with other work and responsibilities. The following comments express this student's attitude: "I can see that the homework is necessary. I just want to find a way to make time for doing it that doesn't kill me. I'm stressed out enough as it is."

We will use Pat's goal of five additional hours per week for homework as the example for each step of the goal-setting model. The goal should not be attempted if any of the following criteria cannot be met in the judgment of the student planning solutions with adults.

1. *Achievability:* Does the student have the necessary skills and knowledge? Is help necessary? If so, how dependable is that help? Is there enough time to reach the goal? (Coincidentally, Pat's problem is time itself. Pat's after-school routine is two hours on part-time job, one hour to travel, one hour to help prepare supper and eat; two hours of homework; one hour to relax and watch TV; and off to sleep at approximately 10:00 P.M. Discussion indicates that there are three possible areas of adjustment—work, TV, and sleep. At this point the goal seems

achievable but not easily so. To gain the hour, Pat plans to cut one-half hour of TV watching and one-half hour of the job.)

2. *Measurability:* How will the student specifically be able to gauge progress or achievement? This can be something as simple as problems completed, pages read, or exercises finished. The main thing is to decide on a way of measuring so that feedback is a tangible reality for self-evaluation. (Pat's situation is simple because time is easy to measure.)

3. *Desirability:* Is the goal something the student really *wants* to achieve? If the goal is forced upon the student, then the self-determination aspect of this process is lost. (Pat is not wild with joy about doing an extra hour of homework each night, but has pride as a learner and wants to do quality work.)

4. *Focus:* Some plan by which the goal is daily placed in the student's awareness is important to avoid forgetting or procrastination. Effective reminders, such as outlines, chalkboard messages, or daily logs, help avoid nagging. (Pat's parents agree to sign Pat's assignments for the next two weeks to indicate the extra hour has been spent. Pat has agreed to log in with them every evening. The teacher has agreed to accept all of Pat's assignments, complete or otherwise, as long as the parent's signature is present. This should aid cooperation because all parties have interdependent responsibilities.)

5. *Motivation:* How is the process of reaching the goal motivating? Whatever is done to attain the goal should have some appeal to the student in order to maintain perseverance, because initial motivation may wear thin. (Pat's parents and teacher are supportive. Pat's participation in class should improve, which should increase Pat's feelings of competence. Fortunately, the way this entire process has been conducted has made doing five extra hours of homework a manageable challenge for Pat.)

6. *Commitment.* Is the goal so valued that the student can make a formal or informal gesture to pledge effort and responsibility? This can be anything from a statement such as "I'm really going to try" to a handshake to a contract. This affirms the student's self-determination and encourages the development of self-respect. (Pat's father comments that the plan looks good

and he'd like to shake on it. With a slightly impish grin, Pat shakes hands.)

If any of the criteria are not met, the goal is in need of alteration or abandonment. If the criteria are met, there is an excellent probability that the goal can be achieved. Two more things can be done:

7. *Identify resources:* The student benefits from knowing where support is possible. This might mean identifying materials, books, tutors, libraries, or any special help to make the goal more achievable. (Pat suggests getting stuck on an assignment is a real possibility and wonders if any help might be available. The teacher agrees to setting up a cooperative relationship with another student so at least telephone assistance is possible.)

8. *Make plans to remove obstacles:* The question for the student is "What do you think might interfere with the achievement of your goal?" This may include anything from other obligations to lack of a quiet place to study. Planning gives the student added leverage to contend with these obstructions and barriers. (Pat's answer is classic: "TV—I know it. As soon as I turn it on, I'm hooked." Pat's parents agree to move the set into another room and monitor it.)

After goal setting has been conducted, the follow-up process is the same as that for problem solving.

Follow-Up on Problems of Insufficient Effort

Encouragement and evaluation of results as discussed in Chapter Six are equally applicable to the plans that resolve insufficient effort. In general, the adults concerned act with the belief and trust that the student will improve his or her effort. A schedule should be established to check progress and to maintain the momentum of the plan. (The first check should occur within one or two weeks at most and with regular intervals thereafter, until all parties agree it is not necessary.) This will allow for fine tuning the development of the plan as well. In this manner, minor distractions can be more easily eliminated. These meetings offer a good opportunity for the adults involved to further encourage the student. When things are going smoothly, the meetings can become briefer and evolve into telephone calls and reciprocal notes until the student's improved pattern of effort seems well established.

As Alex Molnar and Barbara Lindquist have written, sometimes examples in books sound like fairy stories and have the quality of being too good to be true.[3] Pat listens. Pat participates. Pat agrees. Pat increases homework time by five hours. In real life there are glitches, confusion, and a rockier road. Relapses are fairly common when young people attempt to increase their effort. Something else may gain their interest. Old habits reemerge. They just get plain tired. They forget their schedule. There are so many possibilities for things to go wrong. That is why temporary setbacks should be considered normal; they are little reason to become discouraged or blame others. This is the time for adults to help students to reevaluate their plan, make the necessary adjustments, and show support and confidence that the students will improve. It is sometimes a good idea to tell students that such setbacks are a normal and predictable part of change. This helps them to save face, renew their confidence, and avoid giving up because of guilt or fear of ever having another such problem.

Seriously Resistant Students

One of the most difficult situations a teacher or parent may face is when a child has decided to make virtually no effort toward achievement in school. In fact, some children make sure this point is abundantly clear. They want it known that they have no interest in, or intention of, becoming involved in school learning.

Needless to say, this can be very upsetting to parents and teachers, and these situations can escalate quickly into full-blown power struggles. Soon the question "Who will win?" becomes the primary concern, with the issue of academic achievement taking a secondary place. The struggle is paramount and the focus is on the battle itself rather than on why it is being fought.

Breaking this pattern is extremely difficult because of the bind that has been created. Neither party wants to give in and in essence lose face. As time goes on, both dig their heels in ever deeper, and the cost of "losing" seems even greater.

Recognizing the pattern early and making a decision to change it as soon as possible can be a first, and effective, step toward resolution. Parents and teachers who become skilled at this are often able to avert major problems.

Refusing to participate in the power struggle is the key to success in breaking the pattern. How is this done?

The most important point to keep in mind is that what has been tried in the past hasn't worked. More of the same is not likely to solve the problem. (Giving up will not solve it either.) Deciding to take on the challenge of finding another way can be a courageous and rewarding step.

The goal is to change the child's behavior in ways that will allow the child to maintain his or her integrity. Efforts toward humiliation inevitably backfire. Coercion is not likely to work in these cases. Although threats may work in other situations, they usually will not work here.

It is important to look at alternatives and to think creatively. Consider the following approaches; they may lead to more effective solutions.

1. *Ask the young persons how they make* not *doing schoolwork okay in their own minds.* Then determine if there are any ways to cooperate on the basis of reasons such as making time spent with friends more important than doing schoolwork. This may not be a value that adults agree with, but it is not irrational for young people to think this way today. Knowing this is their perception opens the door to further problem solving.

2. *As parents and teachers, consider what might make* not *doing schoolwork acceptable to the students and appear reasonable to us.* For example, scorning school might help a student gain status with a peer group. If this were actually so, one alternative is to discuss the value of membership in the peer group and find a more constructive way to participate in the peer group. These might be possible avenues to solving the problem.

Because these two examples deal with friends and peer groups, we want to emphasize that parental influence on adolescent educational aspirations generally exceeds peer influence and actually *increases* over the high school years.[4] Parents are wise to take an active interest in the friends of their children and to encourage relationships that support the importance of learning at school.

Parents and teachers may need to back off for a while. They might even have to steel themselves to allow the child to live with the consequences of his or her behavior. They probably will need to look at things from a different perspective. They may need to try different methods of communication or new negotiating skills. They may have to learn to accept small steps in progress and subtle signs of improvement.

There are no magic solutions to complex problems such as these, but perseverance and acceptance of the fact that change usually takes time and effort can contribute to creating more positive approaches to problem solving.

If the methods we have recommended do not appear to be helping to improve insufficient effort, we still advocate that parents do not give up. The problem may require a counselor or someone who can give more specialized help. There are also other approaches. We think *Changing Problem Behavior in Schools*, by Alex Molnar and Barbara Lindquist, is exceptional in its creativity and practical suggestions.[5]

To hope for and believe in one's children is very important. The effects are much like a timed-release capsule. They can show up in the years ahead, still potent, although their source is remote. Students who know that their parents and teachers have abiding faith in them carry a reassurance that time seldom wears thin.

Epilogue

—8—

Creating Friendship
Between a Child and Learning

"The best thing for being sad," replied Merlin, beginning to puff and blow, "is to learn something. That is the only thing that never fails. You may grow old and trembling in your anatomies, you may lie awake at night listening to the disorder of your veins, you may miss your only love, you may see the world about you devastated by evil lunatics, or know your honor trampled in the sewers of baser minds. There is only one thing for it then—to learn. Learn why the world wags and what wags it. That is the only thing which the mind can never exhaust, never alienate, never be tortured by, never fear or distrust, and never dream of regretting. Learning is the thing for you."

—Terence H. White, *The Once and Future King*

LEARNING IS HOPE. It summons forth images symbolic of an optimistic destiny: Einstein floating in a galaxy of stars, a blissful child leafing through a book on a spring afternoon, a monk pondering an ancient manuscript in a murky abbey. With learning there is always a future. Most of history is not so much finding a way out of the dark as much as it is learning a way into the light. To be motivated to learn means to carry an enduring disposition that you can know more and make a better contribution to your world.

Writing this book has helped us to learn more clearly than ever before that what makes people want to learn through the channels of reading, writing, thinking, and computing is an ongoing

114

and very vulnerable process. It can be stopped by worry, depression, disease, distraction, failure, boredom, drugs, and anything else that circumstances and experience make more immediately compelling. Motivation to learn is not to be taken for granted. It is the difference between living and existing.

We are convinced that parents make the greatest difference in the development of most people's motivation to learn, and no force is as powerful in rejuvenating a child's motivation to learn as a parent and teacher working in collaboration.

Parents can help their children to establish an identity as learners through their own modeling of a respect for learning and their treatment of their children as capable and lovable people. Teachers do their share by making the process of learning successful, worthwhile, and challenging. Yet they cannot do what parents do, and society is misguided to expect otherwise. Motivation to learn develops in children because parents make it a priority in their families. The evidence for this influence crosses a wide variety of ethnic groups and all socioeconomic classes.

Parents and teachers have a responsibility to contact each other when help is needed in the domain of learning. We see that this works best when the attitude is one of gumption, the feeling is one of trust, and the action taken is one of cooperation.

As we gathered information in preparation for writing this book, we were a bit surprised to find how consistently powerful the role of effort is in almost all aspects of learning. We were intimidated as well. To know that working very hard is the path to excellence was not startling. But the extent to which we found perseverance and exertion crucial to creativity, stimulation, and confidence was somewhat unexpected. Ultimately, we realized that developing motivation to learn as a trait involves embracing discipline and persistence as a way of being, as a form of valued emotional stamina.

Our learning was greatly enhanced and our own effort supported by the realization that depending too much on any outside goal for motivation to learn makes a person more vulnerable to external controlling forces and weakens overall performance. When a student enjoys learning and remains a learner, goals emerge. The goals of learning are born within the act of learning. To make students think the goals of learning are grades contaminates their self-determination and may produce achievement but not learning for the sake of learning, which is the cradle of new knowledge and scientific discovery.

Perhaps the best metaphor for motivation to learn is friendship, a friendship between a person and learning. Friends nurture, help, and value one another. For people, learning is always available, its wisdom is everywhere, and its value is as eternal as life itself. To human beings it is a mighty companion. To foster motivation to learn in young people is to encourage them to enjoy that friendship, to show them what it means in our own lives, to let them have time with books and paper and thinking—time for wonder and worthwhile struggle. Parents and teachers, in friendship, can do this best of all for children.

Resources

Resource A

TEACHER QUESTIONS FOR PARENTS

Dear Parents,

Please take a few minutes to help me get to know your child better by answering these questions. Sharing this information with me will help me prepare for our upcoming conference. All information you share will remain strictly confidential.

Academic Progress

1. What does your child have to say about his or her progress in school? _____

2. In what ways is your child working up to your expectations? _____

3. In what ways is your child not meeting your expectations?_____

4. What does your child like most about school? _____

5. In what one area would you most like to see your child improve this year? _____

6. In your child's opinion, what would make life at school more interesting or enjoyable? _____

7. What aspects of schoolwork does your child consider most difficult? _____

8. What things at school tend to upset your child? _____

Homework and Home-Learning Activities

9. How do you feel about the homework your child is expected to do? _____

10. How does your child react if you help with homework? _____

11. How often do you and your child read together? _____
12. What television programs do you and your child watch together? ___

13. What activities do you and your child especially enjoy doing together? _____
14. How does your child act if you correct a mistake or suggest an area to work on? _____

Home Life and Behavior

15. What types of activities take up your child's leisure time? _____

16. What kinds of chores does your child have at home? _____

17. How does your child handle chores you assign? _____
    _____

18. What does your child do when upset or angry? _____
    _____

19. What observations can you share about your child's relationship with peers? _____
    _____

20. How do you encourage good behavior at home? _____
    _____

21. How much sleep does your child usually get each night? _____
    _____

22. Are there any health, medical, or family concerns that might affect your child's performance in school? _____
    _____

Parent Signature _____

Teacher Signature _____

(All responses confidential—for professional use only)

Note: Questions adapted from R. D. Strom, H. W. Bernard, *Educational Psychology* (Monterey, Calif.: Brooks/Cole, 1982).

Source: Chrispeels, J., Boruta, M., and Daugherty, M. *Communicating with Parents.* San Diego, Calif.: San Diego County Office of Education, 1988, p. 276. Used with permission of the authors and the San Diego County Office of Education.

Resource B

PARENT QUESTIONS FOR TEACHERS

Dear Parents,

We will be meeting soon to talk about your son or daughter's progress and success in school. I am providing you with a list of questions to help you think through what you would most like to know. We won't have time to discuss all these questions at this conference, but circle the ones that are most important to you and let me know which ones they are. Complete and return the tear-off section on page two. Keep the list of questions for your files and bring them to the conference with you.

Sincerely,

_____

(Teacher's Name)

Classroom Behavior

1. How well does my child get along with you? _____
2. How well does my child get along with other students? _____
3. When my child gets angry, how does he/she express it? _____
4. How does my child solve conflicts with others? _____
   With you? _____
5. Does my child bother other children or disturb the class? _____
6. In what ways does my child contribute positively to the class? _____
   _____
7. What ways do you reward good behavior in your class? _____
   _____
8. What are the consequences for misbehavior? _____

Work Habits

9. How does my child behave when working with a group? _____
   _____
10. How does my child behave when he/she is stuck or can't do his/her work? _____
11. How well does my child pay attention in class? _____
12. Do any activities seem to frustrate my child? _____
13. How well does my child stick to a difficult task? _____
14. What activities does my child seem to enjoy most in school? _____
    _____

Academic Progress

15. What does my child really do well? _____
16. Does my child recognize this strength? _____

17. In terms of grade level how is my child doing in:
     Reading ___ Writing ___ Math ___ Social Studies ___ Other___ ?
18. What do you take into account in deciding grades? _____
     _____
19. What does my child need to work on most? _____
20. How can I help? _____
21. In what ways is my child working up to your expectations? _____
     _____
22. In what ways is my child not working up to your expectations? _____
     _____

Homework

23. What kind of homework help do you expect us to provide? _____
     _____
24. How much time should my child be spending on homework? _____
25. How often do you assign homework? _____
26. Does my child complete homework assignments on time? _____
27. What are the consequences for incomplete or late homework? _____
     _____
28. Is homework graded, and are those grades used and reported? _____
     _____

___ I am looking forward to our conference on _____ at _____ .
                                              (date)   (time)
___ I am unable to attend at the time you have scheduled for me. The best
    times for me are _____ or _____ .
                       (date and time)   (date and time)
The five questions I most need answers to are # ____ , ____ , ____ , ____ ,
and ____ .

_____
(Parent Signature)

Source: Chrispeels, J., Boruta, M., and Daugherty, M. *Communicating with Parents.* San Diego, Calif.: San Diego County Office of Education, 1988, p. 274. Used with permission of the authors and the San Diego County Office of Education.

Resource C

PARENT WORKSHEET TO PREPARE FOR PARENT-TEACHER CONFERENCE

Child's Name: _____
Teacher's Name: _____   Room Number: _____
Conference Date: _____   Time: _____

I. Please complete this section at home before the conference.

   A. What I think my child does well at home: _____
   _____

   B. What I think my child does well in school: _____
   _____

   C. One problem I would like to discuss with the teacher: _____
   _____

   D. Questions I would like to ask: _____
   _____
   _____
   _____

II. Action Plan: Ways the teacher and I can work together to help my child. (Complete this section with the teacher at the conference.)

   A. What the teacher will do at school: _____
   _____

   B. What I will do at home: _____
   _____

   C. How we will check our progress (notes, telephone calls, etc.):
   _____

Source: Chrispeels, J., Boruta, M., and Daugherty, M. *Communicating with Parents.* San Diego, Calif.: San Diego County Office of Education, 1988, p. 279. Used with permission of the authors and the San Diego County Office of Education.

Resource D

PARENT CHECKLIST FOR CONFERENCING WITH A CHILD'S TEACHER

Before the conference

_____ Write or call to make or confirm my appointment.

_____ Use the material given to me to prepare for the conference.

_____ Talk with my child about his/her school (discuss successes, achievements, favorite subjects, problem areas, etc.).

_____ Review my child's work that he/she has brought home.

_____ Think about child's level of achievement and my expectations for my child.

_____ On conference worksheet or a piece of paper, note concerns and questions about child's work, classroom, or school program.

_____ Share with the teacher, in advance, the most urgent items I need to discuss.

_____ Decide with my child and the teacher if my child is going to be included in the conference.

_____ Find out how much time has been allotted and decide what is most important to discuss in the time available.

_____ Organize someone to babysit or ask the school to provide child care so that I can be free to concentrate on the conference.

_____ Ask a friend to come if I feel I need help or support.

_____ Ask for a translator, if necessary.

_____ Arrive on time!

At the conference

_____ Say something positive to the teacher to help us both feel more comfortable.

_____ Decide with the teacher what is most important to talk about.

_____ Refer to my notes and questions so I will not forget any important issues.

_____ Take notes during the conference.

_____ Ask questions and make sure I understand all that the teacher is saying.

_____ If my child is at the conference, make sure we listen to him/her.

_____ Summarize what has been said.

_____ Write down a plan of action that says what the teacher and I will do.

_____ Let the teacher know how best to reach me and decide how I will communicate with the teacher (call, notes, future conferences).

_____ Thank the teacher for his/her time and concern.

After the conference

_____ Share with my child what was discussed at the conference.

_____ Do what I said I would do.

_____ Through a note or telephone call, let the teacher know how things are going.

Source: Chrispeels, J., Boruta, M., and Daugherty, M. *Communicating with Parents.* San Diego, Calif.: San Diego County Office of Education, 1988, pp. 277-278. Used with permission of the authors and the San Diego County Office of Education.

Resource E

NARRATIVE PUPIL PROGRESS REPORT

ENCINITAS UNION SCHOOL DISTRICT
Narrative Pupil Progress Report
School Year _____

Name of Pupil _____ Grade _____ Teacher _____
Date of Report _____ School _____
_____

Immediate Goals: Assignment for Next Year _____
_____

Language Arts: (Reading, Spelling, Handwriting, Reference Skills, Oral &
_____ Written Expression)
_____

Math:
_____

_____

Social Science:
_____

_____

Science & Health:
_____

_____

Special Subjects: (Art, Music, & Physical Education)
_____

_____

Teacher Comments:
_____

Personal Development—	Responsibility	☐ Is considerate of others.
O, S, N, U	☐ Accepts responsibility for	☐ Shows self-control.
O—Outstanding	actions.	☐ Respects authority.
S—Satisfactory	☐ Cares for property.	☐ Is cooperative.
	☐ Assumes responsibility for	☐ Shows good sportsmanship.
N—Needs to improve	assigned tasks.	
U—Unsatisfactory	☐ Abides by school rules.	Work Habits
		☐ Listens to and follows
	Attitudes	directions.
	☐ Accepts suggestions and	☐ Completes assignments on time.
	criticisms.	☐ Works well with others.
		☐ Works independently.

Source: Chrispeels, J., Boruta, M., and Daugherty, M. *Communicating with Parents.* San Diego, Calif.: San Diego County Office of Education, 1988, p. 164. Used with permission of the authors and the San Diego County Office of Education.

Resource F

STUDENT INTEREST SURVEY: A TOOL FOR TEACHERS

Because student interests change so rapidly and because youth is more and more a culture unto itself, this survey offers a convenient way to collect some practical information about your students' current interests. Such information is helpful for making subject matter more relevant as well as giving new insights to the many ways there are to relate to students.

Directions:

For students who can read and write at the fourth-grade level and above, you can duplicate and distribute the survey for written completion. The students are to complete this form honestly and sincerely but without publicly sharing the information in order to avoid influencing their peers. Indicate to the students that this information will be used to better understand ways to make their learning more positive and important for them. The students are not to be concerned about any academic judgment regarding the spelling or grammar of their responses. They will need about fifteen minutes to finish the task. If students object or refuse to complete certain items, their rights are to be respected. None of the information on an individual survey should be shared without the student's permission.

For students who read and write below the fourth-grade level, a personal interview or group discussion regarding each item may be necessary to gather the information. There is also the possibility of simplifying the language on some of the items and offering individual assistance where necessary. In general, the teacher can supplement and improvise any item as the situation merits.

The sentence-completion items are never to be considered as absolutes and, in some instances, may be meaningless or misleading. Personal discussion with the student is one of the best ways to gain clarification. After gathering the student surveys, examine them for any trends such as the most popular movie or favorite TV program and consider making up a class profile and sharing it in discussion with your students. Students will find this appealing because it deals with their identity and things they value.

After you have organized the information collected in the survey, consider the following questions:

1. What new information did you learn about your students?
2. Was there anything in the survey results that surprised you? Pleased you? Made you feel uncomfortable?

Often it is helpful to list the ways you might use some of this information for instructional purposes such as new projects and subject-related examples based on the students' interests.

Student Interest Survey

Date: _____   Student Name: _____

1. The best movie I've recently seen is _____ .
2. A reward I like to get is _____ .
3. My two favorite TV programs are _____ .
4. One thing I do very well is _____ .
5. My favorite school subject is _____ .
6. When I read for fun I like to read stories about _____
    _____ .
7. If I had ten dollars, I'd spend it on _____ .
8. When I have free time I like to _____ .
9. I enjoy _____ .
10. If I could go anywhere, I would go to _____ .
11. One of the things I like best about myself is _____ .
12. A good thing my teacher could do for me is _____ .
13. My favorite game is _____ .
14. An important goal for me is to _____ .
15. I know a lot about _____ .
16. Sometimes I worry about _____ .
17. I spend most of my money on _____ .
18. The thing I most like to do with my friends is _____ .
19. I like it when my parents give me _____ .

Annotated References

Part One

1. Tough, A. *The Adult's Learning Projects*. (2nd ed.) Austin, Tex.: Learning Concepts, 1979.

Chapter One

1. This consistently documented finding in psychology has a long tradition. White, R. W. "Motivation Reconsidered: The Concept of Competence." *Psychological Review*, 1959, *66*, 297-333.

2. Some experts cite the basic design of the graded school as a trap that snares both teachers and students into a system of constant testing and labeling that inevitably leads to failure, especially for the at-risk students. Cuban, L. "The 'At-Risk' Label and the Problem of Urban School Reform." *Phi Delta Kappan*, 1989, *70*, 780-801.

3. Home environment and quality of instruction have been identified as at least two of the crucial factors that mutually interact to influence student progress in learning. Thus a point of diminishing returns in learning is prone to be flexible and temporary when such factors can be positively increased. Walberg, H. J., and Uguroglu, M. "Motivation and Educational Productivity: Theories, Results, and Implications." In L. J. Fyans, Jr., (ed.), *Achievement*

Motivation: Recent Trends in Theory and Research. New York: Plenum, 1980.

4. Human beings are inherently active. Our minds are constantly vigilant, surveying the environment, focusing and changing our attention. Such efforts tend toward spontaneity rather than stable concentration. The dynamic qualities of these processes contribute to our species' adaptability and survival. Deci, E. L., and Ryan, R. M. *Intrinsic Motivation and Self-Determination in Human Behavior.* New York: Plenum, 1985.

Chapter Two

1. The Asian/Pacific American label represents a very diverse group, including Chinese, Japanese, Korean, Filipino, Vietnamese, Thai, Cambodian, Laotian, Indonesian, and discrete ethnic groups from Pacific islands too numerous to mention. There is some evidence that the high academic achievement reported for this overall group is due to cultural influences affecting primarily second- and third-generation children. Morishima, J. K. "Academic Characteristics of Asian/Pacific Americans." In W. J. Lonner and V. O. Tyles, Jr. (eds.), *Cultural and Ethnic Factors in Learning and Motivation: Implications for Education.* From the 12th Western Symposium on Learning, Western Washington University, Bellingham, 1988.

2. However, personal achievement and competing with others are not emphasized as reasons for attaining academic success. White, M. *The Japanese Educational Challenge: A Commitment to Children.* New York: Free Press, 1987.

3. Research shows not only that the Japanese emphasis on effort is pervasive but that they also have constructed a reward system, evaluation system, and other structures in school to consistently carry out this value. Holloway, S. D. "Concepts of Ability and Effort in Japan and the United States." *Review of Educational Research,* 1988, *58,* 327–345.

4. For more than twenty years, research has shown that students from the elementary level through high school benefit from family conditions and practices that emphasize and encourage learning in school. Henderson, A. *The Evidence Continues to*

Grow: Parent Involvement Improves Student Achievement. Columbia, Md.: National Committee for Citizens in Education, 1987.

5. Bloom, B. S. *Developing Talent in Young People.* New York: Ballantine, 1985.

6. His initial research conducted with poor families in Chicago is available in book form. Clark, R. M. *Family Life and School Achievement: Why Poor Black Children Succeed or Fail.* Chicago: University of Chicago Press, 1983.

7. Clark, R. M. "Effective Families Help Children Succeed in School." *Network for Public Schools,* 1987, *13* (1), 1-5. Published by the National Committee for Citizens in Education, Columbia, Md.

8. Clark, R. M. " Effective Families . . . ," pp. 1-5.

9. As such, teachers are not merely reactors to whatever motivational patterns their students have developed before entering their classrooms but also can be directly influential, capable of developing student motivation to learn in particular situations. Brophy, J. "Synthesis of Research on Strategies for Motivating Students to Learn." *Educational Leadership,* 1987, *45* (2), 40-48.

10. Larkins, A. G., McKinney, C. W., Oldham-Buss, S., and Gilmore, A. C. *Teacher Enthusiasm: A Critical Review.* Hattiesburg, Miss.: Educational and Psychological Research, 1985.

11. Brophy, J., and Good, T. L. "Teacher Behavior and Student Achievement." In M. C. Wittrock (ed.), *Handbook of Research on Teaching.* (3rd ed.) New York: Macmillan, 1986.

12. Good, T. L., and Brophy, J. *Educational Psychology.* (3rd ed.) New York: Longman, 1986.

13. Brophy, "Synthesis of Research on Strategies," pp. 40-48.

14. Crooks, T. J. "The Impact of Classroom Evaluation Practices on Students." *Review of Educational Research,* 1988, *58,* 438-481.

15. Crooks, T. J. "The Impact of Classroom Evaluation . . . ," pp. 438-481.

16. Crooks, T. J. "The Impact of Classroom Evaluation . . . ," pp. 438-481.

17. Brophy, "Synthesis of Research on Strategies," pp. 40-48.

18. This quality is critical to enhancing intrinsic motivation

among students. Deci, E. L., and Ryan, R. M. *Intrinsic Motivation and Self-Determination in Human Behavior.* New York: Plenum, 1985.

19. This includes a realization of student misconceptions. Porter, A. C., and Brophy, J. "Synthesis of Research on Good Teaching: Insights from the Work of the Institute for Research on Teaching." *Educational Leadership,* 1988, *45* (8), 74–85.

20. Crooks, "The Impact of Classroom Evaluation . . . ," pp. 460–481.

21. In the 1986–87 school year, U.S. public schools administered at least 105 million standardized tests. Neill, D. M., and Medina, N. J. "Standardized Testing: Harmful to Educational Health." *Phi Delta Kappan,* 1989, *70,* 688–697.

22. This list is based on the research reported in their seminal article about the development of self-regulation in children. Ryan, R. M., Connell, J. P., and Grolnick, W. S. "When Achievement Is *Not* Intrinsically Motivated: A Theory of Self-Regulation in School." In A. K. Boggiano and T. S. Pittman (eds.), *Achievement and Motivation: A Social-Developmental Perspective.* Cambridge: Cambridge University Press, forthcoming.

Chapter Three

1. These researchers stress that the typical outward signs of motivation, such as concentration or achievement, may not be as important as the adolescent's inner motivational thoughts about the meaning of effort and the relationship of effort to self-worth. Ames, R., and Ames, C. "Adolescent Motivation and Achievement." In J. Worell and F. Danner, (eds.), *The Adolescent as Decision Maker.* Orlando, Fla.: Academic Press, 1989.

2. Dornbush, S., and others. "The Relation of Parenting Style to Adolescent School Performance." *Child Development,* 1987, *58,* 1244–1257.

3. An outstanding resource for developing an authoritative approach to classroom discipline: Curwin, R. L., and Mendler, A. N. *Discipline with Dignity.* Alexandria, Va.: Association for Supervision and Curriculum Development, 1988.

4. Smith, F. "Overselling Literacy." *Phi Delta Kappan,* 1989, *70,* 358.

5. Paulos, J. A. *Innumeracy.* New York: Hill and Wang, 1989.

6. This book describes a wide array of learning activities that parents can participate in with their children (ages four to twelve) to develop their motivation to learn. Rich, D. *Megaskills.* Boston: Houghton Mifflin, 1988.

7. Csikszentmihalyi, M., and McCormack, J. "The Influence of Teachers." *Phi Delta Kappan,* 1986, *67,* 415-419.

8. Covington, M. V., and Omelich, C. L. "It's Best to Be Able and Virtuous Too: Student and Teacher Evaluative Responses to Successful Effort." *Journal of Educational Psychology,* 1979, *71,* 688-700.

9. Supportive of this notion is the fact that Japanese pre-schools and elementary schools emphasize social competence and physical development in their curriculum. They believe later academic achievement and professional accomplishment are ensured through the development of perseverance and commitment. Holloway, S. D. "Concepts of Ability and Effort in Japan and the U.S." *Review of Educational Research,* 1988, *58,* 327-345.

10. Csikszentmihalyi, M., and Nakamura, J. "The Dynamics of Intrinsic Motivation: A Study of Adolescents." In C. Ames and R. Ames (eds.), *Research on Motivation in Education.* Vol. 3. Orlando, Fla.: Academic Press, 1989.

11. Most learning mistakes are not random. They are usually logical and have a pattern. Gage, N. L., and Berliner, D. C. *Educational Psychology.* (4th ed.) Boston: Houghton Mifflin, 1988.

12. Researchers have found that parents of extremely talented and successful young people tend to have given consistent support at home for *any* educational ambitions, including music, science, and sports. Bloom, B. S. *Developing Talent in Young People.* New York: Ballantine, 1985.

13. Kulik, C-L. C., and Kulik J. A. "Mastery Testing and Student Learning: A Meta-Analysis." *Journal of Educational Technology Systems,* 1987, *15,* 325-345.

14. Good, T. L., and Brophy, J. *Educational Psychology.* (3rd ed.) New York: Longman, 1986.

15. Good and Brophy, *Educational Psychology.*

16. Good and Brophy, *Educational Psychology.*

17. Henderson, A. *The Evidence Continues to Grow: Parent Involvement Improves Student Achievement.* Columbia, Md.: National Committee for Citizens in Education, 1987.

18. Almost all parents can be effectively involved in learning activities at home when their children are in grade school. Epstein, J. L. "Parents' Reactions to Teacher Practices of Parent Involvement." *Elementary School Journal,* 1986, *86,* 277–294.

Chapter Four

1. Jaynes, J. H., and Rugg, C. A. *Adolescents, Alcohol, and Drugs.* Springfield, Ill. Thomas, 1988.

2. There is evidence that in many families poor grades trigger child abuse. Toufexis, A. "Report Cards Can Hurt You." *Time,* May 1, 1989, p. 75.

3. Deci, E. L., and Ryan, R. M. *Intrinsic Motivation and Self-Determination in Human Behavior.* New York: Plenum, 1985.

4. Skinner, B. F. "Why Teachers Fail." In R. C. Sprinthall and N. A. Sprinthall (eds.), *Educational Psychology: Selected Readings.* New York: Von Nostrand Reinhold, 1969.

5. Weiner, B. *Human Motivation.* New York: Holt, Rinehart & Winston, 1980.

6. Natriello, G. "The Impact of Evaluation Processes on Students." *Educational Psychologist,* 1987, *22,* 155–175.

7. When norm-referenced evaluation procedures are used, it is impossible for large numbers of students to experience academic success. Covington, M. V., and Beery, R. G. *Self-Worth and School Learning.* New York: Holt, Rinehart & Winston, 1976.

8. Crooks, T. J. "The Impact of Classroom Evaluation Practices on Students." *Review of Educational Research,* 1988, *58,* 438–481.

9. Good, T. L., and Brophy, J. *Educational Psychology.* (3rd ed.) New York: Longman, 1986.

10. Japanese high school students spend up to forty hours in extramural tutoring and study per week, in addition to regular school on Saturday and only brief summer vacations. Walberg, H.

J., Paschal, R. A., and Weinstein, T. "Homework's Powerful Effects on Learning." *Educational Leadership,* 1985, *42* (7), 76–79.

11. Critical to the future of this society and especially its young people is the development of the awareness and pursuit of enjoyment in productive activities. Csikszentmihalyi, M., and Csikszentmihalyi, I. (eds.) *Optimal Experience: Psychological Studies of Flow in Consciousness.* New York: Cambridge University Press, 1988.

12. Research studies find that the teacher, the parents, and the student jointly determine the actual benefits of homework. Walberg, Paschal, and Weinstein, "Homework's Powerful Effects," pp. 76-79.

13. Merrow, J. "Children and Television: Natural Partners." *Phi Delta Kappan,* 1985, *67,* 211–214.

14. Aronson, S. S. "Ensuring Your Child's Healthy Future." *Pediatric News,* January 1989, p. 28.

15. Aronson, "Ensuring Your Child's . . . ," p.28.

16. Liebert, R. M., and Sprafkin, J. *The Early Window: Effects of Television on Children and Youth.* (3rd ed.) New York: Pergamon, 1988.

17. Also recommended by Action for Children's Television.

18. Atkinson, J. W. "Motivational Effects in So-Called Tests of Ability and Educational Achievement." In L. J. Fyans, Jr. (ed.), *Achievement Motivation: Recent Trends in Theory and Research.* New York: Plenum, 1980.

19. Peng, S. S., Fetters, W. B., and Kolstad, A. J. *High School and Beyond: A National Longitudinal Study for the 1980s.* Washington, D.C.: National Center for Education Statistics, 1981.

Part Two

1. Lipsitz, J. *Successful Schools for Young Adolescents.* New Brunswick, N.J.: Transaction Books, 1984.

Chapter Five

1. Ashton, P. T., and Webb, R. B. *Making A Difference: Teachers' Sense of Efficacy and Student Achievement.* New York: Longman, 1986.

2. The problem is not in conflicting views over the value of

education but rather in parents' and teachers' misperceptions of one another. Lightfoot, S. L. *Worlds Apart: Relationships Between Families and Schools.* New York: Basic Books, 1978.

3. An excellent, practical, and labor-saving collection of strategies and materials designed to help schools and teachers communicate better with parents. Chrispeels, J., Boruta, M., and Daugherty, M. *Communicating with Parents.* San Diego: San Diego County Office of Education, 1988.

Chapter Six

1. Bloom, B. S. *All Our Children Learning.* New York: McGraw-Hill, 1981.

2. Weiner, B. "Principles for a Theory of Student Motivation and Their Application Within an Attributional Framework." In R. E. Ames and C. Ames (eds.), *Research on Motivation in Education: Student Motivation.* Vol. 1. Orlando, Fla.: Academic Press, 1984.

3. Gagné, R. M., and Smith, E. "A Study of the Effects of Verbalization on Problem Solving." *Journal of Experimental Psychology,* 1962, *63,* 12–18.

4. These researchers found the following responses to be generally *ineffective* when parents use them to improve the poor grades of their children: ignoring, yelling or getting upset, promising extrinsic rewards such as car use for higher grades, and punishment. Most helpful was encouragement. Dornbush, S., and others. "The Relation of Parenting Style to Adolescent School Performance." *Child Development,* 1987, *58,* 1244–1257.

5. Mastery learning is an instructional strategy that allows students to study material until they can demonstrate that they have competently learned the material. Students are allowed more time, usually through some form of sequential tasks, to master material instead of being pushed ahead to new material. Bloom presents data to suggest that 80 percent of students reach an achievement level that fewer than 20 percent of these students would attain under nonmastery conditions. He argues that under mastery conditions it is possible for almost all students to master most of the material in present school curricula. Bloom, *All Our Children,* pp. 131–175.

6. Bloom, *All Our Children,* p. 173.

Chapter Seven

1. In general, the more students perceive their learning as due to outside pressure and the quest for extrinsic rewards, such as test scores leading to promotions, the less they will find the act of learning rewarding in itself. Deci, E. L., and Ryan, R. M. *Intrinsic Motivation and Self-Determination in Human Behavior.* New York: Plenum, 1985.

2. Hill, K., and Wigfield, A. "Test Anxiety: A Major Educational Problem and What Can Be Done About It." *Elementary School Journal,* 1984, *85,* 105–126.

3. Spielberger, C., Anton, W., and Bedell, J. "The Nature and Treatment of Test Anxiety." In M. Zuckerman and C. Spielberger (eds.), *Emotion and Anxiety: New Concepts, Methods, and Applications.* Hillsdale, N.J.: Erlbaum, 1976.

4. Dusek, J. B. "The Development of Test Anxiety in Children." In I. G. Sarason (ed.), *Test Anxiety: Theory, Research, and Applications.* Hillsdale, N.J.: Erlbaum, 1980.

5. Hill and Wigfield, "Test Anxiety," pp. 105–126.

6. Results of 562 studies were integrated by meta-analysis to show the nature, effects, and treatment of academic test anxiety. Hembree, R. "Correlates, Causes, Effects, and Treatment of Test Anxiety." *Review of Educational Research,* 1988, *58,* 47–77.

7. The volume of testing in schools has been increasing by between 10 percent and 20 percent annually over the past forty years. Almost every large educational reform effort of recent years has mandated either a new form of testing or expanded uses of existing testing. Learning and teaching are corrupted when most of the instruction becomes merely preparation for testing. Haney, W., and Madaus, G. "Searching for Alternatives to Standardized Tests: Whys, Whats, and Whithers." *Phi Delta Kappan,* 1989, *70,* 683–687.

8. Hill, K. T., and Sarason, S. B. "The Relation of Test Anxiety and Defensiveness to Test and School Performance over the Elementary School Years." *Monographs of the Society for Research in Child Development,* 1966, *31* (2, serial no. 104).

9. Hill and Wigfield, "Test Anxiety," pp. 105–126.

10. Hill and Wigfield, "Test Anxiety," pp. 105–126.

11. Covington, M. V. "The Motive for Self-Worth." In R. E.

Ames and C. Ames (eds.), *Research on Motivation in Education: Student Motivation.* Vol. 1. Orlando, Fla.: Academic Press, 1984.

12. Hill and Wigfield, "Test Anxiety," pp. 114-126.

13. Zatz, S., and Chassin, L. "Cognitions of Test-Anxious Children under Naturalistic Test-Taking Conditions." *Journal of Consulting and Clinical Psychology,* 1985, *53,* 393-401.

14. Hill and Wigfield, "Test Anxiety," pp. 114-126.

15. Hill and Wigfield, "Test Anxiety," pp. 114-126.

16. Hill and Wigfield, "Test Anxiety," pp. 111-126.

17. Hill, K. T. "Debilitating Motivation and Testing: A Major Educational Problem—Possible Solutions and Policy Applications." In R. E. Ames and C. Ames (eds.), *Research on Motivation in Education: Student Motivation.* Vol. 1. Orlando, Fla.: Academic Press, 1984.

18. Dr. Kennedy T. Hill, 210 Education Building, University of Illinois, 1310 S. Sixth St., Champaign, Ill. 61820.

19. Hembree, "Correlates, Causes, Effects, and Treatment," pp. 47-77.

20. Hembree, "Correlates, Causes, Effects, and Treatment," pp. 47-77.

Chapter Eight

1. Davies, D. R., Shackleton, V. J., and Parasuraman, R. "Monotony and Boredom." In R. Hockey (ed.), *Stress and Fatigue in Human Performance.* New York: Wiley, 1983.

2. Csikszentmihalyi, M. *Beyond Boredom and Anxiety: The Experience of Play in Work and Games.* San Francisco: Jossey-Bass, 1975.

3. Davies, Shackleton, and Parasuraman, "Monotony and Boredom," pp. 1-32.

4. Kerman, S. "Teacher Expectations and Student Achievement." *Phi Delta Kappan,* 1979, *60,* 716-718.

5. Marzano, R. J., and others. *Dimensions of Thinking: A Framework for Curriculum and Instruction.* Alexandria, Va.: Association for Supervision and Curriculum Development, 1988.

6. Teachers can be helpful to students taking notes by making sure their presentation rate is not too fast. Mayer, R. E. *Educa-*

tional Psychology: A Cognitive Approach. Boston: Little, Brown, 1987.

7. A common problem is that students often underline or highlight too much. In general, it is better to be selective. In studies that place a limit on how much students can underline—for example, only one sentence per paragraph—learning has improved. Snowman, J. "Learning Tactics and Strategies." In G. Phye and T. Andre (eds.), *Cognitive Classroom Learning: Understanding, Thinking and Problem Solving.* Orlando, Fla.: Academic Press, 1986.

8. Many such elaborating strategies are especially effective with low-achieving students. Marzano and others, *Dimensions of Thinking,* pp. 101–103.

9. Csikszentmihalyi, M., and Nakamura, J. "The Dynamics of Intrinsic Motivation: A Study of Adolescents." In C. Ames and R. E. Ames (eds.), *Research on Motivation in Education: Goals and Cognitions.* Vol. 3. Orlando, Fla.: Academic Press, 1989.

10. Professor Cross emphatically makes the case that the single most important goal for educators at all levels and in all agencies is the development of lifelong learners, who possess the basic skills for learning plus the motivation to pursue a variety of learning interests throughout their lives. Cross, K. P. *Adults as Learners: Increasing Participation and Facilitating Learning.* San Francisco: Jossey-Bass, 1981.

11. Gage, N. L., and Berliner, D. C. *Educational Psychology.* (4th ed.) Boston: Houghton Mifflin, 1988.

12. Brophy, J. "Synthesis of Research on Strategies for Motivating Students to Learn." *Educational Leadership,* 1987, *45* (2), 40–48.

13. In fact, the more unexpected the event, the greater the arousal from it. Apter, M. J. *The Experience of Motivation.* Orlando, Fla.: Academic Press, 1982.

14. This method is based on the research and theory of the eminent cognitive scientist Jean Piaget. He and his colleagues provided evidence that the essential functional need that motivates us is cognitive disequilibrium, which is the tension we feel when we experience something that does not fit what we already know. This tension causes us to involve ourselves with the new experience in

order to understand it. Sigel, I. E., Brodzinsky, D. M., and Golin-koff, R. M. (eds.). *New Directions in Piagetian Theory and Practice.* Hillsdale, N.J.: Erlbaum, 1981.

15. An excellent professional resource for educators who want to develop creative and critical thinking among their students. Marzano and others, *Dimensions of Thinking.*

16. Corno, L., and Mandinach, E. B. "The Role of Cognitive Engagement in Classroom Learning and Motivation." *Educational Psychologist,* 1983, *18* (2), 88–108.

17. Crooks, T. J. "The Impact of Classroom Evaluation Practices on Students." *Review of Educational Research,* 1988, *58,* 438–481.

18. Wlodkowski, R. J. *Enhancing Adult Motivation to Learn: A Guide to Improving Instruction and Increasing Learner Achievement.* San Francisco: Jossey-Bass, 1985.

19. All the theory and research cited in this section is refer-enced and discussed in this comprehensive resource. Johnson, D., and Johnson, R. T. *Learning Together and Alone: Cooperative, Competitive, and Individualistic Learning.* (2nd ed.) Englewood Cliffs, N.J.: Prentice-Hall, 1987.

20. Deutsch, M. "Cooperation and Trust: Some Theoretical Notes." In M. R. Jones (ed.), *Nebraska Symposium on Motivation.* Lincoln: University of Nebraska Press, 1962.

21. Johnson, D. W., and Johnson, R. T. *A Meta-Analysis of Cooperative, Competitive, and Individualistic Goal Structures.* Hillsdale, N.J.: Erlbaum, 1987.

22. Johnson and Johnson, *A Meta-Analysis.*

23. Johnson, D. W., and Johnson, R. T. "The Socialization and Achievement Crisis: Are Cooperative Learning Experiences the Solution?" In L. Bickman (ed.), *Applied Social Psychology Annual 4.* Newbury Park, Calif.: Sage, 1983.

24. For a much more thorough discussion of how to struc-ture cooperative learning, see Johnson and Johnson, *Learning To-gether and Alone,* pp. 43–63.

25. Johnson and Johnson, *Learning Together,* pp. 1–194.

26. Slavin, R. *Cooperative Learning.* New York: Longman, 1983.

27. Ryan, R. M., Connell, J. P., and Grolnick, W. S. "When

Achievement Is *Not* Intrinsically Motivated: A Theory and Assessment of Self-Regulation in School." In A. K. Boggiano and T. S. Pittman (eds.), *Achievement and Motivation: A Social-Developmental Perspective.* Cambridge: Cambridge University Press, forthcoming.

28. Csikszentmihalyi and Nakamura, "The Dynamics of Intrinsic Motivation," pp. 51–71.

29. Csikszentmihalyi and Nakamura, "The Dynamics of Intrinsic Motivation," pp. 51–71.

30. Csikszentmihalyi and Nakamura, "The Dynamics of Intrinsic Motivation," pp. 51–71.

31. Springsteen, B. "No Surrender." From *Born in the U.S.A.*, 1984. Used with permission.

Chapter Nine

1. Covington, M. V., and Beery, R. *Self-Worth and School Learning.* New York: Holt, Rinehart & Winston, 1976.

2. Costa, A. L. "Mediating the Metacognitive." *Educational Leadership,* 1984, *42* (3), 57–62.

3. Molnar, A., and Lindquist, B. *Changing Problem Behavior in Schools.* San Francisco: Jossey-Bass, 1989.

4. Exceptions to this general finding were in some cases deviant where peer group pressures were unusually strong and consistent, or where communication between parents and their children had broken down. Davies, M., and Kandel, D. B. "Parental and Peer Influences on Adolescents' Educational Plans: Some Further Evidence." *American Journal of Sociology,* 1981, *87,* 363–387.

5. Molnar and Lindquist, *Changing Problem Behavior.*

Index